THE DON'T SWEAT GUIDE
TO YOUR FINANCES

Other books by the editors of Don't Sweat Press

THE DON'T SWEAT GUIDE TO YOUR FINANCES

Planning, Saving, and Spending Stress-Free

By the Editors of Don't Sweat Press
Foreword by Richard Carlson, Ph.D.

New York

ISBN: 1-4013-0759-0

Hyperion books are available for special promotions and premiums.
For details contact Michael Rentas, Manager, Inventory and Premium Sales,
Hyperion, 77 West 66th Street, 11th floor, New York, New York 10023,
or call 212-456-0133.

FIRST EDITION

10 9 8 7 6 5 4 3 2 1

Contents

Foreword

Most people agree that personal finances can be stressful at times. There is so much to keep track of: investments, taxes, paperwork, changes in the law, credit card and bank statements. It is also important these days for all of us to pay close attention to security issues, such as keeping our personal information private to avoid identity theft. There are so many bills to pay, and even with the Internet, there are piles of paper everywhere!

Discipline in our spending is also critical but not always easy. It's important and often difficult to live within one's means. With so much consumption temptation at our fingertips and all over the media, it can be hard to set a ceiling on our desires. Everywhere we turn, something seems to be calling out to us, "Buy me." Everyone else seems to be able to afford so much, and if they can't, they simply get another line of credit. We ask, "Why shouldn't I do that?"

There's another reason that finances are important, and that has to do with social responsibility. The more responsible, ethical, and organized that we are with our own finances, the more comfortable we will be in giving our money away to organizations that we believe in.

The editors of Don't Sweat Press have written what I think is an excellent guide to the world of finances. Unlike many stale and often boring guides, filled with facts and figures, this book includes the much-needed missing link—perspective. The book shows you some creative ways to keep your cool in the midst of chaos and clutter and ways to manage your decisions and keep track of everything, all without losing your bearings.

I believe that this book can make the difference in keeping the stress of finances from becoming overwhelming. Often, a slight shift here or a small change in attitude there can be all the difference it will take to keep things under control.

To me, the key to finances, as in most other aspects of life, is to keep a clear mind that is not distracted by frustration, stress, and irritation. In the absence of distraction, you have what it takes to get the job done.

I've never believed that money is the most important part of life, and I hope you don't, either. However, there's no denying the fact that if we deal with our finances responsibly, ethically, and in an organized fashion, we will be less stressed as a result. I hope this book serves you in helping to create this reality, as it has for me.

Richard Carlson
Benicia, California, 2004

THE DON'T SWEAT GUIDE
TO YOUR FINANCES

1.

Setting Financial Goals

Most people have financial goals that they want to achieve; however, quite often they fall short of those goals. Make certain that you achieve your goals by following these four easy steps.

First, visualize your goal. As easy as this sounds, this is very important. Clearly imagine and describe your goal in positive terms. For instance, don't say that you want to cut spending by fifteen percent. Instead, state the goal in terms of saving $350 a month. You can save this money from your paycheck in a proactive manner. Then you can determine how you are going to reduce your spending in order to save the money. While the positive goal gets you to the same place, saving $350 a month sounds better than reducing spending by fifteen percent. After all, who wants to have a negative goal to meet?

When you have your goal, write it down. The more specific it is, the easier it is to attain it. Read your goal each day in order to focus your mind on it.

The next important thing to do is to give yourself a deadline. Without a deadline, the goal is nothing more than a good idea. Everyone has good ideas; unfortunately, it takes more than a good idea to accomplish a goal.

The remaining step is to stay focused. As easy as that seems, it really isn't. As soon as you make a resolution to accomplish a goal, circumstances will conspire to move you away from your goal. For instance, you may be invited to travel with your friends on a ten-day cruise that is the best bargain ever at $799; or, as bad luck would have it, your television may break, leaving you to spend $500 on a new one.

Life will conspire to get you off the track of attaining your financial goals. However, you don't have to give in to the temptation or the perceived urgency of spending. After all, your financial future is at stake. Stay focused, and hold on to your goal.

2.

Access Your Home's Riches

The smart homeowner will want to fully utilize the home's riches by obtaining a credit line based on the equity in the home. A home-equity credit line is an easy way to pay for purchases using borrowed money with a low interest rate while being able to deduct the interest expense from your income taxes. The credit line can be used to pay for remodeling the kitchen or redecorating the entire house. College education expenses, a special vacation, or car purchases are other popular expenditures that a home-equity credit line can fund. Many people also use home-equity credit lines to pay off high-interest credit card balances.

To put the power of a home-equity credit line to work for you, call your mortgage lender to find out what the current interest rate and fees are. Then call other banks to find out what their terms are. After doing your homework, you will know what bank is offering the best deal.

It is important to remember that a home-equity credit line isn't just for spending. It also can be obtained and reserved for emergency use. That way, if a financial catastrophe occurs, funds are readily available. While some banks may charge a small fee for the credit line, interest isn't charged unless money is actually borrowed. The peace of mind that an open credit line provides more than justifies the small fee.

However, as the saying goes, there is no free lunch. Remember that any borrowed funds eventually have to be paid back. Don't take on more debt than you can afford. If your financial circumstances change—for example, if you lose your job—failing to pay your home-equity credit line could mean that the bank could seize your home in a foreclosure proceeding. Also, if you plan to sell your home and buy a bigger one, the bank will use the sale proceeds to pay off your credit line, as well as the mortgage. Your large windfall that you anticipated to pay for the new home could be a lot smaller than you originally had thought.

Home-equity credit lines can be a valuable financial tool. Just make certain that you are aware of the downside, as well as the benefits.

3.

Accounting Made Simple

If you ever thought that accounting was complicated, think again. There's no reason that accounting has to be difficult if you understand a few simple concepts. With that knowledge, you can grasp the basics of accounting. Soon, you'll be able to maneuver your way around even the most complex financial statements.

There are three major documents that comprise a company's financial statements: an income statement, a balance statement, and a statement of cash flows. Each statement gives you unique information.

The income statement summarizes a company's revenues and expenses. To simplify, if you subtract expenses from sales, you will see how much money the company made, which is its net income. Once the net income is calculated, it is divided by the number of shares outstanding, which gives you the basic earnings per share.

The balance sheet says nothing about how much the company made or lost. Instead, it explains how many assets the company owns, as well as how much debt it has. If investors are concerned that a company has too much debt, then they will closely watch the balance sheet to see if the debt is growing or decreasing. Assets listed will include current assets—cash, accounts receivable, inventories, and prepaid expenses—as well as other long-term assets, such as equipment, land, and buildings. If the company has assets such as goodwill, those will be listed. Also listed on the balance sheet is stockholders' equity, which shows how much of the owners' money is invested in the company.

The third report is the statement of cash flows. This measures how much money is coming into the company and what it is being used for, as well as how much money the company has used and where that money went. This is important, because even if a company is profitable, if outgoing money exceeds incoming money, the company could still run into trouble.

Once you learn a few accounting basics, you can add to your knowledge until you obtain mastery of the subject. Eventually, you'll be reading through statements in a matter of minutes. After all, shouldn't investing give you time for a better quality of life without intimidating you with the details?

4.

Clarity Creates Money

If you listen to any conversation between friends, you will hear complaints that they aren't paid enough, have too many bills, or wonder why their money doesn't go further. While everyone has concerns about money, don't shortchange yourself. Take the time to clarify the positive aspects about your financial situation, as well as the negatives. This will allow you to take positive actions to improve the quality of your life and help you fulfill your financial goals.

Clarity gives you the inner peace of knowing what your financial strengths and financial weaknesses are. Often, people don't give themselves credit for what they have and instead focus on the negatives. For instance, people with large credit card debts may feel like they have failed. At the same time, they are ignoring the fact that they earn $80,000 a year. While that doesn't make them millionaires, it does mean that they have a nice income, and they should be proud of themselves.

If you are looking at your checking account balance to determine how you are doing financially, that is perhaps the wrong place to look. Instead, total up your savings and brokerage account balances, and add in the value of retirement accounts and the equity in your home. Once all of those numbers are added together, you might find that your opinion of your financial situation improves.

Clarity is also important to allow you to clearly identify what you don't like about your financial situation and develop a plan to make the appropriate changes. Money should be available to add to your quality of life. If you have clarity about what you have or don't have, you can make an informed decision about what changes you need to make. For instance, if you have not set aside enough for retirement, you can take the constructive actions needed to remedy the situation instead of just worrying about it. Those actions will increase your peace of mind and boost your self-confidence.

Clarity lets you remove the fear of the unknown and set yourself on a path to achieving constructive financial goals. Once fears—rational or irrational—are brought into the light of day, they won't seem so overwhelming.

5.

Be a Smart Home Buyer

Purchasing a home can be one of the most stressful financial events in a person's life. In order to manage your workload and head stress off even before it begins, start the process to become pre-approved for a mortgage.

Pre-approval provides several advantages. First, when you meet sellers, they know that they are dealing with someone who can complete the transaction. That keeps a deal from falling apart because the potential buyer couldn't obtain financing. If you are in a situation where there may be several parties that are putting in bids on a house, you want to be in the dominant situation of letting the seller know that you have already been approved for a mortgage. Even if your offer is slightly lower, if the seller knows that the deal will be completed, you have a distinct advantage.

By talking with your bank first, you will quickly find out if you are looking at houses that are too expensive for your financial circumstances. Sometimes, a reality check can be helpful, and obtaining that earlier in the process is important.

Another advantage of being pre-approved for a mortgage is that you can quickly discover any lurking credit problems and resolve those early in the process. By finding out the bad news earlier, you'll have plenty of time to resolve any problems.

You also might save a significant amount of money. For example, a credit problem may not be sufficient enough to prevent you from receiving a mortgage. However, it may result in a higher interest rate, which over the life of a thirty-year mortgage will cost you thousands of dollars. By having plenty of time to resolve the problem or provide an explanation, you may be able to still receive the lowest interest rate possible.

Purchasing a house is stressful enough. Take care of yourself, and adopt the best financial practices by obtaining pre-approval for your mortgage. By taking care of it ahead of time, you can keep your stress level to a minimum and focus on completing the house purchasing process.

6.

Beat Credit Card
Companies at Their Game

Every week, millions of people are bombarded with offers to sign up for credit cards. The offers often end up in the trash—the result of our confusion about which card company to choose and why. In our busy lives, sorting through all the information just seems too time-consuming.

The competitive battle among credit card companies desperate to attract the best customers does mean a better opportunity for credit-worthy customers. Here are some simple guidelines to follow to make sure that you profit from this situation in order to obtain the least expensive credit card with the most perks.

As you receive these offers in the mail, collect them over several weeks, and then compare them to see which card offers the lowest interest rate for the longest period of time. You may even receive a credit card that charges no interest for one year!

For people who are carrying a balance on their credit card, such offers can be particularly lucrative. Many cards offer an interest rate of zero for a specific time. This allows you to transfer your balance from a high-interest credit card to a card that charges no interest, which will save a significant amount of money and help you pay the balance off much more quickly.

If you have offers for several cards that charge no interest, examine how much you will be charged for transferring a balance to that card. Often, the fee is equal to three percent of the balance being transferred, with a cap set at thirty-five or fifty dollars. If you know that you can pay the card balance off before the no-interest-rate period expires, then the card offering the lowest balance transfer fee will be your best option. However, if you won't be able to pay it off during that time period, you are better off taking the card with the longest period of zero-percent interest, even if the balance transfer fee is more.

Also look at the length of a grace period on purchases, which often is twenty-five days. If a card seems to offer the lowest interest rate but has no grace period for purchases, it might not be the best deal in the long run, because interest charges begin accumulating even before you have received the bill.

It's worth a little bit of time to research credit cards to ensure that you receive the best deal. After all, why pay more interest and fees than are necessary?

7.

Buy the Best House
That You Can Afford

When interest rates are at low levels, homebuyers have an amazing discount available to help them take care of their families and provide a secure home. With low mortgage interest rates, the smart buyer will take advantage of the situation to buy the nicest house possible.

However, just because you may have the ability to make your money go farther doesn't mean that your goal is to keep up with the Joneses. Nothing could be further from the truth. Instead, you'll be taking advantage of the fact that houses are on sale and have the opportunity to provide more for your family now than ever before.

Here's how it works. When interest rates fall, the amount of monthly mortgage payments declines drastically, as well. That means the $250,000 house that you were eyeing would go on sale, opening up two options. First, your $250,000 house would cost less than it once would have, saving you considerable money in the process. Second, with the substantially lower cost, maybe you could purchase a house for $275,000 instead.

It also is possible to lower the monthly mortgage payment even further. A variable-rate mortgage will have a lower interest rate than a thirty-year fixed mortgage, passing along savings and lowering your monthly payment. However, variable mortgages require caution. The interest rate will be guaranteed for a period of three or five years, and then it can change. If interest rates rise, your monthly payment will rise, too.

You must make these decisions with an eye toward your future. That said, it can be difficult to project where you will be in five or ten years' time. Just because you are able to spend more now doesn't mean that you should. Examine your motivations. Are you caught up in what your friends are doing? As human beings, we are susceptible to want to "keep up," but if you make keeping up a priority, nothing can bring on more stress than suddenly finding yourself unable to do so.

Make certain that you carefully evaluate how expensive a house you can afford. While you may be able to purchase something much nicer than you ever dreamed, you don't want to end up in a financial bind and create more problems for your family.

8.

Check Your Credit Report

One of the most effective ways to preempt a stressful situation when purchasing a house or car is to find out ahead of time what your credit report says. That simple action will avoid unpleasant surprises when you are ready to make a large purchase.

While you may think that your credit is perfect, a mistake could have been made by one of the credit reporting agencies. A creditor also could have accidentally attributed a negative comment about someone else to your credit report. Mistakes do happen.

Even if there are no mistakes, the report may mention late bill payments that you weren't aware were on your report. If it does, you should have a response prepared. Obtaining your credit report before you need it gives you the time to prepare a response. For instance, if one credit card company reports that you have paid your bill late, you can prepare an explanation about what happened. You can point out that this was an insolated instance and show the other times that you have paid your bills on time.

However, if there was a pattern of late bill payment, you may have had extenuating circumstances. If you were sick for an extended period of time, or if you were laid off and your unemployment benefits didn't cover all of your expenses, you can explain that situation so your potential creditors understand that it was a difficult and extraordinary time. You can show that you paid your most important expenses, such as your rent and car payment, and had to juggle other bills, such as credit cards. You also can point out that as soon as you were employed or healthy again you began paying all of your bills on time.

Finding out exactly what your credit report says before anyone checks it can substantially reduce your stress level. If your credit rating is perfect, then you can relax knowing that you won't have any problems obtaining credit. Instead, you will be viewed as a perfect buyer, making the purchase process as stress-free as possible.

9.

Choosing a Bank

It is important that you determine what you need in a bank and then choose accordingly. Some people hate to pay monthly fees for checking accounts, even if they are just five or ten dollars per month. If that sounds familiar, you will want to ask, in advance, what a bank's checking account charges will be. Usually, that involves knowing what balance you are likely to keep in the checking account and knowing what will be charged if your balance drops below that level.

Along those lines, perhaps the bank that offers you the ability to have your checking and savings accounts, individual retirement accounts (IRAs), credit cards, and mortgage all at the same place might be the most appropriate. If the total assets in your account can be used to calculate your minimum balance, that is a good feature to have. If this helps you stay organized and manage your finances, it is even better.

Another item to evaluate is whether the bank has a national presence. This may be particularly helpful if you tend to travel a lot. That way, you aren't continually getting stuck with fees from ATMs. If it is likely that you will move several times, you may want a bank with a national presence so that you don't need to transfer all of your accounts.

If you are attempting to save time, you will probably want to make certain that your bank has either a telephone bill payment service or online banking service that lets you pay bills and monitor your account anytime using the Internet. There are actually a handful of banks that have sprung up during the last several years that do nothing but provide online banking. These banks are attractive to new depositors because they typically pay higher interest rates on deposits in order to win new customers. If you believe in maximizing your ability to earn every possible dollar, then you will probably want to explore using such a bank.

Banks now come in many different shapes and sizes and offer customers a much wider variety of services from which to choose. Maximize your time and money, and select the bank that will do the most for you.

10.

Choosing an Online Stockbroker

If you want to open up a trading account with an online discount broker, begin gradually by purchasing a few stocks to see if you are pleased with the service. Continue doing this for a series of trades to see if any glitches arise. That will give you time to determine if the web site is easy to use and understand.

You may want to test how responsive the company is by sending an e-mail inquiry and observing how quickly your question is answered. Also, call the firm a few times to see how long you are kept on hold. It can be extremely frustrating if your question or problem can't be handled online. Make certain that you still have access to a live person.

Next, investigate what free news, stock quotes, and research you can receive. Just because you are using an online discount broker doesn't mean that you shouldn't have a variety of services and information available. One thing that brokerage firms increasingly do is offering seminars to their customers on topics such as investing or saving for retirement.

The web site also should have online tools that help you identify your investment style and narrow down your investment options. Does the site offer you tools to compare different stocks? These types of tools can make your investment decisions significantly easier than using traditional stock selection methods. If you need more help, does the discount broker provide experts who will help you? If so, find out what minimum account size is required to be eligible for this service.

Finally, some discount brokerages are part of a larger bank which has its accounts insured by the Federal Deposit Insurance Corporation (FDIC) up to $100,000. The advantage of using a discount brokerage owned by a bank is that idle funds not invested in stocks or bonds can be invested with the bank and be insured by the federal government. However, this does not insure the value of the stocks or bonds that are purchased for the account. Those still face the potential danger of declining significantly.

Discount brokerages have made it much easier for many people to actively invest in the financial markets, and there is no reason why you should not be one of the beneficiaries. Just take your time to investigate the service and make certain that your needs are met.

11.

Free Money from Your Employer

As strange as this seems, millions of Americans turn down free money from their employers, because they neglect to put money aside into their company's 401(k) plan. Quite often, those contributions are matched at least partially by employers. Because many people don't participate in a 401(k) plan, they aren't eligible to receive the matching funds.

Some people believe that they can't spare the extra money from their paychecks to invest in a 401(k) plan. However, on closer examination, you aren't giving up much extra money at all. For example, if you set aside ten percent of your salary into your 401(k), your net pay doesn't decrease by ten percent, because your contribution lowers the amount of your salary that is taxed. You will barely notice the "missing" money, because the taxes withheld from your paycheck decrease. If you don't contribute to your 401(k) it is like passing up a tax cut, in addition to passing up free money.

Some companies match your contribution up to three or four percent of your salary. Other companies may match your entire contribution. Whatever the matching amount is, take it.

Still, there is one cautionary note for people who tend to change jobs frequently. While your employer may match your contribution, you don't fully own that money until you are vested. Companies typically have vesting periods of four or five years. For example, if your company has a four-year vesting period, each year, you would have a right to hold on to twenty-five percent of your employer's matching contribution. If you leave the company after two years, you will only be able to keep fifty percent of the matching contributions. Of course, any contribution that you make yourself is completely owned by you and remains your property if you change jobs.

As tight as money may seem today, visualize thirty or forty years down the road when you are retired. Would you rather live without a few dollars today when you are working or have to face finding a job at age seventy? With that in mind, take your employer's money and start securing your retirement.

12.

Complete Your Taxes
in Two Hours or Less

Why agonize and spend hours poring over your income tax returns when you can accomplish the task in two hours or less? With online tax filing or an income tax software program, your taxes can be completed quickly while you receive expert advice at the same time.

Once you receive your W-2 form, which shows what you earned, and your 1099 forms, which show the amount of interest and dividends that you received, you can go online and find a tax filing web site. Before choosing one, however, you may want to compare some of these to some of the major tax software programs available to discover which ones likely will work the best for you. Also, you can use the Internet to access reviews of tax filing programs.

Once you've decided which tax filing system is right for you, you can either purchase the software in a store and install it on your computer or go to the web site and begin the process of entering your information. Even if you don't understand the entire process of filing out the return, the software or web site will guide you and ask you specific questions that you can answer. The software or web site will act as a consultant and can provide assistance when you have questions.

Additionally, either of these systems will avoid addition or subtraction mistakes that can be made using pencil and paper. While that may sound like a minor point, many taxpayers actually shortchange themselves by making mathematical errors.

An added bonus to using a filing site on the Internet or a software-based filing program is that you can opt to file your return electronically once it is completed. Then you can have your refund direct-deposited into your checking account, further speeding up the process.

There's no reason why paying taxes has to be difficult now that technology has created such easy-to-use tools. Save time and money by unleashing the power of computers to help you complete your financial chores.

13.

Discussing Your Expectations

In a marriage, or when two people decide to live together, what one person does with his or her money substantially impacts the other person and often obliterates his or her financial plans. While you are excited about creating a life together, make certain you are taking the steps to create a solid foundation for the future by discussing your financial expectations before embarking upon a long-term relationship. As in the case of religion, lifestyle, number of children, and numerous other issues, financial goals must be discussed. If the differences are too drastic, then the relationship is going to have a very hard time surviving.

Both people in a relationship want to have a loving, fulfilling life together and remain committed to each other. Unfortunately, financial problems are one of the biggest reasons couples split up. Don't let that happen to you. By discussing your financial expectations beforehand, you can avoid financial arguments later on and take constructive actions to create a loving life together.

There are several areas that are good places to start. Examine your and your partner's attitudes toward debt. For instance, is carrying any credit card balance okay? If so, how much? If one person explodes each time a credit card bill with a balance shows up in the mail, arguments will result. What about debt on a home equity line of credit? Is this acceptable debt? If so, what amount is acceptable?

Beyond regular monthly expenditures, you will probably want to discuss retirement goals. While it may be perfectly obvious to you that the maximum should be contributed to a 401(k) plan, your future partner might have different ideas. Don't wait for problems to arise. Discuss your expectations today.

Another area that people often argue about is monthly savings. If one person wants to save the maximum amount of money possible, and the other partner comes home having spent three hundred dollars at the mall, problems will result. It also is important to discuss whether those savings are to remain in the bank for a rainy day or are to be used to pay for a large vacation. Create the foundation for a loving relationship by taking the time to clarify your financial goals and expectations.

14.

Create Simplicity with a Computer

Half the battle of getting your finances under control is having the appropriate information available so that you can make the right financial decisions. One way to do that is to use a personal finance software program. Many programs also help you set financial goals and calculate how long it will take to reach those goals.

Probably the best feature about using a personal finance program is that all of your financial information is at your fingertips. Once you've entered the information in the software program, it will produce dozens of financial reports that you can use.

Software programs can help you answer the question, "How much money do I have?" This doesn't just include what is in your checking account. It includes your savings, brokerage, and 401(k) accounts. Also covered is the value of any assets such as houses, other real estate, or other personal property such as cars.

Software also can quickly tell you how much money you owe. In order to come up with this calculation, your credit card balances, car loans, and the amount of your mortgage outstanding are calculated. The amount of what you owe is subtracted from your assets, which quickly gives you your net worth.

Once you have the appropriate information, you can make some informed decisions. Do you need to pay off debt? Do you need to save more money? After you have decided what your goals are, the software will outline what you need to do to reach them. If one goal is to set a realistic budget, the software gives you the ability to set up a budget and then track your spending against it.

Remember, if you really want to get your finances under control, the first step is to have the appropriate information available so that you can make the right decisions. Using a personal financial software program will give you that information so you can take control of your finances and develop the financial life that you truly want.

15.

Create Opportunity
from Being Laid Off

While being laid off is probably one of the most frightening financial events in a person's life, it is possible to turn adversity into opportunity. Faced with an unexpected layoff, you quickly have to make decisions about what you are going to do. If you ever thought that you might want to do something different, now is the time to jump at the opportunity. After all, you no longer have the security of a job to stop you from doing something that you really want to do.

Not surprisingly, some people decide that they really want to help others and decide to become therapists, nurses, members of the clergy, or nonprofit administrators. Those who want to become teachers may find that this option is much easier than it ever was. School districts, especially in inner cities, often make it relatively easy for college-educated professionals to transition into teaching jobs without having to go back and obtain teaching degrees.

Others may find that they are attracted by much more self-serving plans, which is perfectly fine. If you always wanted to be a ski bum, your opportunity has arrived. Ski resorts have plenty of jobs available that will allow you to pay your bills, as long as you don't plan on living in the most expensive condo in town.

Some people know that they are in the right field but may decide to take a two-month-long vacation and travel to far-flung corners of the world. After all, when are you ever going to have this much time to travel again? Retirement is probably the next opportunity and that's a long way off.

If you've been laid off, take the opportunity to create the life that you really want, not the life that you believe you are supposed to have. After all, life is not a dress rehearsal and there are no encore performances. Carpe diem!

16.

Deciding on Bankruptcy

Determining whether to file bankruptcy is a stressful decision that has to be carefully weighed with your best interests in mind. Whatever choice you make will have a serious and lasting impact on your finances for at least seven years while that information sits on your credit report. However, the ongoing strain of paying back all of the money that you owe may be too much to cope with.

Before reaching your decision, the most important thing to consider is your own emotional well-being and peace of mind. While you must consult attorneys and other professional advisors before making any determination, you alone have to evaluate whether filing for bankruptcy will better alleviate your pressure and emotional stress or whether you would be more empowered to pay your debts.

Filing for bankruptcy can lead some people to feel as if they have failed. If you make the decision to file for bankruptcy, it is helpful to recognize that you may have these feelings and learn how to combat them. Filing for bankruptcy takes great courage and is clearly a plan of action. It is a business decision, and you are taking care of your business. It also should help to remember that many great financial wizards have, at one time or another in their lives, been in the same position that you are. There is no shame in taking stock of your situation and concluding that you need assistance. To the contrary, taking control of your life can lead to self-respect and empowerment.

If you are confused about your decision, you'll want to realistically determine whether there is any way that you will be able to pay your debts. To do this, list all of your debts and the amount of monthly payments, and make a note about the interest rates that you are paying. Then calculate a scenario of how long it will take you to pay those bills with any extra cash that you have each month. When making the calculation, don't forget about other potential income streams, such as an income tax refund or a bonus from your job.

Can you tap any cash sources to pay your bills, such as a savings account? What about using a new, low-interest credit card to consolidate your bills so that you can pay them off more quickly? Another strategy to investigate is borrowing against your 401(k) retirement account. This should be employed carefully, as you are putting your retirement assets and your future quality of life at stake. Also, don't forget that you will need several thousand dollars to pay for a bankruptcy filing in order to pay attorney's fees and court costs.

After careful consideration, you may opt for bankruptcy. Remember, the best decision is the one that takes care of you in the best way possible.

17.

Create a Budget

There's nothing worse than worrying about money every day. Financial difficulties detract from your quality of life and cause unnecessary stress. Fortunately, there is an easy answer. Create a spending plan, otherwise known as a budget. This doesn't have to be complex. It can be as easy as making a shopping list, which is a stress-free activity.

A budget is a means to an end and keep in mind that the end you are seeking is empowering yourself to get your spending under control and make certain that you have enough money to lead the life that you envision for yourself and your family.

To start the budget process, determine your total monthly income. This probably will be your net pay from your job but also could include income from a second job or hobby. Now you know the total amount of money that you have available to spend and have completed the first step toward making a budget.

Next, list your mandatory expenses each month, such as rent, car payment, and utility bills. Then list other expenses that are discretionary, such as entertainment, clothing, and charitable donations. Total up the mandatory and discretionary expenses, and see where you are. Hopefully, you have some money left over. If you don't, go back through your numbers and see what expenses you can pare back. Through a little bit of preparation, you can take the steps today to make certain that you aren't spending too much money tomorrow.

Budgets are not just useful for controlling spending. They also allow you to set aside some money for savings. That way, if you have an unexpected expense, you will have some cushion.

Don't cheat yourself. Make certain that you are doing everything possible to create as many opportunities to provide for yourself and your family. If a budget will add to the quality of your life and reduce your stress, what are you waiting for?

18.

Dig Yourself Out of Debt

Even with the best intentions, we sometimes end up slipping further and further into debt. Once you realize that you have a problem, you can begin to take constructive steps to tackle that pile of debt and get rid of it. Remember, don't beat yourself up. Everyone makes mistakes. You should congratulate yourself for taking steps to tackle a problem that has been brewing for some time.

Make a comprehensive list of all of your debts, the monthly minimum payment, the due date, and the interest rate that you are paying. While debts include your mortgage and car loans, those debts are backed by assets, which many don't consider to be "bad" debt. Typically, your list will include credit cards and student loans.

Now you have several options. First, determine how long it would take you to pay off these debts using your available cash. Perhaps by cutting some of your other expenditures, you could free up available cash to pay these bills over the next year. If you can totally pay everything off within a year, that may be your best option.

If you don't want to wait a year, or it will take significantly longer than a year to wipe your debt out, a different tactic is required. You will want to look for a source of cash that you can put toward paying off the debt. This may be money in a savings account, a home equity line of credit, a loan or gift from a family member, a loan from your 401(k) plan, or the consolidation of bills on a low-interest credit card.

Obviously, if you've borrowed money from a 401(k) plan or home equity credit line or put the balances onto a low-interest credit card, you still have debt. The reason that you are using these options is to lower your interest rate so that you can pay your debt off more quickly. Also, with one bill to pay each month, you have the advantage of having a clear reminder of how much money you owe, rather than having the balances spread across many bills that may mask the overall problem.

After you've paid off your debts, the last thing that you want to do is let them build again. Take the time to develop a monthly budget that includes money to pay your bills, as well as to set aside a little bit for savings.

19.

What Does a Mutual Fund Cost?

Depending on your mutual fund, you could be paying a lot more in fees than you realize. To protect yourself, read the fine print in the prospectus where all of the fee information is explained so that you know what you are paying.

The first thing to realize is that there are no-load funds and load funds. "Load" is another term for a sales charge. Fees of load funds often are easier to compare because they are more obvious. For instance, if a mutual fund has a sales load of four percent, for every dollar that you invest, four cents will go to the person and firm selling you the fund. Immediately, you have to earn at least four percent to cover the sales charge. Other types of mutual fund load fees are rear-load, or reverse-load. This means that the fee is deducted when you redeem the shares, not when you purchase the shares.

While most people realize that they are being charged these fees, they often don't notice the other fees that they are paying. These may be grouped under the heading of "annual fund operating expenses." Typically, this fee is stated as a percentage of the fund's assets and is deducted from the fund. This fee will be separated into three categories. Management expenses often represent the biggest part of the fee and include investment advisory fees, the cost of maintaining accounts, and other administrative expenses such as accounting and legal expenses. Management expenses range from 0.5 percent of the fund's assets up to several percentage points.

A second type of operating expense is a 12b-1 distribution fee. This is the amount of money that goes to the person who sold you the mutual fund. It also covers the cost of sales materials, such as brochures. Funds also will have a line item for "other expenses" that they may or may not charge.

If you invest in mutual funds, you'll want to understand what fees you will have to pay. Next, you'll want to compare these fees among different mutual funds. While you won't necessarily want to pick the mutual fund with the lowest fee, you want to know that if your mutual fund has one of the largest fees, it is justified by the fund's outsized returns.

20.

Do What You Can Do

Financial experts advise people to take a number of positive actions to implement the best financial practices and thus ensure their financial security and stability. With this premise in mind, it becomes your job to weed through all of the "right" recommendations and decide what you can do and what you can't. Whatever you do, don't feel bad about what you can't accomplish. Instead, focus on what you can do.

For example, we are told to make the maximum contributions into our IRAs. That's a great idea, if you can afford it. However, with the contribution limits of 401(k) accounts rising, it may make more sense to put all of your retirement funds into your 401(k) account and ignore the IRA. If your employer has a generous match, such as six to eight percent of your annual salary, then the amount of money that you need to contribute may be even less.

Another piece of advice is to sock away six months of living expenses in case you lose your job. That is a really good idea, and while it might be something that you eventually want to do, it may not be possible today. Instead of six months of living expenses, perhaps you can accumulate three months' worth. You also can determine other actions that you might take in the event that you lose your job. For instance, perhaps you have a friend or family member with a business, such as a restaurant, who could employ you part-time, allowing you plenty of time to look for another job.

Alternatively, you can determine what type of severance benefits you are likely to receive and how much your unemployment benefit is likely to be. While having six months of expenses tucked away is a great idea, don't take that suggestion at face value. Instead, figure out how much money you actually would need after taking inventory of your other resources.

Much of the financial advice that you hear is good. If you can take the good practices and adapt them to your own specific circumstances, you will probably be helping yourself and your finances.

21.

Save for College Now

Achild born this year will have to pay an average of $127,000 in tuition to attend a public university when he or she starts college in seventeen years. That's a staggering amount of money, and the only way to cope with paying that bill is to start saving now. As soon as you apply for your newborn's Social Security card, seriously consider opening up a savings or brokerage account for your child and depositing a few dollars in it. With $127,000 to save, you will need to utilize every year possible in order to build your account by letting compound interest go to work for you.

Fortunately, the government has created several tax-advantageous methods to make saving for college easier. One of the most popular is the 529 College Savings Plan, which lets family and friends invest money for a child's college education. The dividends and capital gains can build without having to pay federal taxes. Some state plans also allow their residents to deduct their contributions from state income taxes. Withdrawals are tax-exempt if they are used to pay for qualified education expenses such as tuition, books, and room and board.

All states offer 529 College Savings Plans, and accounts can be opened through a brokerage firm or another financial service company that sells a state-sponsored plan. An advantage of 529 plans is that they allow an individual to contribute up to $11,000 a year, or $22,000 per couple, which is considerably more than many previous government plans to promote college savings allowed.

Another way to save for college is through a prepaid college plan, which allows parents to prepay up to 100 percent of a child's future college education. For instance, if you pay $8,000 today, that would be the equivalent of paying 100 percent of the annual tuition at the state university in the future. If that tuition is expected to be $30,000 a year, then that may produce a great savings. One drawback for these plans is that your child may not want to go to a state university, or you may have moved to another state by then. There is limited ability in these plans to switch from one university to another. Also, these plans won't pay for tuition at private universities if your child is accepted.

Whatever you do, it's important to begin saving for college now. Who has a spare $127,000 to spend?

22.

Avoid Foreclosure

If you run into financial problems, your home is probably the last thing that you want to lose. Cars, boats, or other consumer items can be sold and later repurchased relatively easily. That's not true for a house. If you realize that you are in danger of losing your home, take action to protect yourself.

One of the first actions is to call your mortgage lender and see what you can do to work out an alternative payment plan. For instance, if you have been unable to pay your mortgage because you have been disabled or lost your job, your lender may be willing to suspend your payments for several months to give you time to get back on your feet. Alternately, the lender may agree to change the terms of the mortgage to reduce the payment. Lowering either the interest rate or the principal portion of the payment or extending the length of the mortgage may accomplish this by reducing the monthly payment and giving you breathing room.

Remember, your lender doesn't want your home any more than you want to give it up. Both parties obviously have incentives to reach common ground. Chances are that the situation may not be as gloomy as you believe.

If you can't work something out with the lender, seek out the services of a bankruptcy attorney or other financial professional who can advise you about the legal actions that you can take to protect your home. If the bank does intend to foreclose on your home, there are many legal steps that have to be taken. This gives you room to negotiate or come up with the money that you need to prevent the foreclosure. Other professionals may be able to help you, as well. Some lenders specialize in home refinancing in order to stop a foreclosure or to buy a home that has already been foreclosed upon. Former mortgage bankers also have set up their own businesses to advise clients on how to stop foreclosure proceedings.

Don't worry—the situation isn't as hopeless as it seems. The U.S. government protects the rights of its citizens, even if they do run into difficulties. Take the situation in hand and take all of the necessary steps to protect your house. You worked too hard to purchase it. Don't let a few temporary setbacks take your home away.

23.

Hire an Expert for Your Taxes

Quite often taxpayers end up cheating themselves out of money that they are owed, because they make mistakes when filing their income taxes. Don't let your innocent mistakes make you overpay or miss a deduction. Instead, hire a professional tax preparer or a certified public accountant (CPA) to do your taxes. While you will have to pay a small amount of money, you will benefit from having a professional complete the task.

A professional preparer can help you in several ways. First, because a tax preparer probably has a staff, several eyes will review your tax return. If there are any mistakes made, the preparer's checks-and-balances system will detect those errors before they get out the door. Few individuals in a hurry to complete their tax returns will be as diligent.

One of the most noticeable ways that individuals cheat themselves is by not taking all of the deductions that they are allowed. Often, business expenses, such as newspaper or magazine subscriptions, professional association dues, or professional meeting expenses that employers don't pay for aren't deducted. A tax preparer can guide you on what expenses you can legitimately deduct. An initial conversation with a tax preparer often turns up expenses that should have been deducted all along, but weren't.

The other advantage of hiring a tax professional is that it is his or her full-time job to keep up with changes in the tax laws, which occur frequently. It is unrealistic for a time-strapped professional with a busy personal life to be fully informed about such a technical topic as income taxes. If you hire a tax professional and are audited, you immediately will have someone on your team who can advise you on how to respond.

Give yourself peace of mind and reduce your income tax stress by hiring a professional. After all, you don't act as your own doctor or car mechanic. Why should you attempt to keep on top of the changing tax laws? Let a tax professional do what he or she is good at while you concentrate on what you are good at.

24.

Organize Your Financial Information

Keep your financial information organized so that you know exactly where you stand at any point. Establish a place for bills that need to be paid, bank statements, and insurance and other financial documents. When you have a question, you can immediately find the document that will give you the answer and remove any chance of confusion.

Sound complicated? It's not. It is very simple. If you can remember where your toothbrush or shirts go, you can organize your financial information. Your financial situation is important. Make life easy for yourself and put your financial documents where you can easily find what you need when you need it. Doing so will greatly reduce the stress surrounding your financial life.

Probably the most important thing to do is to designate one area where you will put your bills that need to be paid. When your paycheck arrives, you can quickly find the bills and write the checks. It's bad enough to have to pay bills. Don't make the job worse by having to hunt for a bill when you misplace it.

Once you've finished paying a bill, it is a good idea to save the bill. If you need to call the company during the month, you have all of the contact information. In the case of credit cards, you should retain the receipts and bills in case you have to return something to the store. Establish one area where you will keep paid bills. Small accordion files are ideal for this task. There is little reason to save utility, cable, and phone bills for more than several months, unless you are deducting them as a business expense on your income taxes. However, if you like to file and retain papers, go right ahead.

Additionally, you will want to have a place designated for other financial documents such as bank statements. A desktop file that can go on a shelf or in a closet may work well. If you have a filing cabinet, statements can go in a hanging file. This also is a good place in which to put other documents, such as insurance statements.

Instead of being confused by your financial information, take control of the situation and organize it. You'll be glad that you did.

25.

Don't Spend Tomorrow's Paycheck Today

If you want to create stress by constantly being worried about how much money is in your checking account, just spend your next paycheck before the funds are even deposited in your bank account. It's the fastest route to creating a downward spiral where you are always broke—even on payday.

Consider whether your spending is worth the resulting stress. After all, how important and fun are shopping trips or social gatherings after work if you have a financial hangover later? Really analyze your spending patterns and determine how much value they are providing. Odds are that the purchases don't justify the stress.

Fortunately, there is an easy solution to eliminating the stress of spending what you have before you have received it. Determine when your major bills are due, such as the rent or car payment. Make sure that the money is available to pay for those important expenses on time. Then list the approximate due dates of your other monthly expenses. Match this information to the dates when your paychecks are issued. This will tell you when you have money to spend and when you need to count your pennies and skip a few trips to the snack bar.

Keep a spending journal for one week to see where all of your money is going. It may surprise you, but lunch, trips to the bookstore, or even a relatively inexpensive evening out may be consuming more money than you imagined when added together. If that spending leads to a constant worry about money because your paycheck is spent before it arrives, then the purchases can't possibly be worth it. If the idea of keeping a journal for a week is too overwhelming, then track your expenditures for just a day or two. Even a few days will provide you with some important insights on how you are spending your money.

To really cut down on stress, save money out of each paycheck for those unexpected expenses. It may be twenty-five, fifty, a hundred dollars, or more, but have some cash set aside so that when you do have an important expense, you have the money to pay for it.

26.

Don't Touch That 401(k)!

When you leave your job, you may think that you've received a financial windfall from your employer's 401(k) retirement plan. After all, one of your options for dealing with the money is to withdraw the cash. However, that is the last thing that a smart investor should do.

For instance, if you have $50,000 in a 401(k) plan and you want to cash it out, almost half of that money will disappear. The federal government will take a ten percent penalty, or $5,000, and depending on your tax rate, about $15,000 will be withheld to pay for federal taxes. If your state or local government has an income tax, the amount of cash that you see could shrink further. All of a sudden, your $50,000 has turned into $30,000, or less.

Not only has your money shrunk, you've lost a tremendous opportunity to gain funds for retirement. By leaving the $50,000 invested for another thirty years until you retire, assuming that you earn eight percent a year, your $50,000 would turn into $546,787.

Once you retire, you may consider the $546,787 to be significantly more important than that $30,000 is today.

There are plenty of other investment options for your 401(k). First, you can leave the money with your former employer, if it amounts to a minimum amount, which typically is $5,000. You can also roll it over into your new employer's 401(k) plan or into your own IRA.

What if you take out only a small amount, such as $5,000? You would have to pay a ten percent—or $500—penalty. Then you would have to pay thirty percent—or $1,500—in taxes, which would give you only $3,000. However, that is only half of the cost. If you left that $5,000 in a retirement account and it earned eight percent a year, in thirty years, you would have $54,679 available for retirement. Thus, the true cost of withdrawing that money amounts to $56,679 after you add in the $2,000 in taxes and penalties that were paid. When you analyze the numbers, it doesn't appear to be a very wise spending decision.

It may seem tempting to get your hands on your 401(k) money now, but don't do it. You will be spending your retirement money and jeopardizing your future financial security. What expenditure could possibly be worth that cost?

27.

Don't Do Everything Yourself

You alone are responsible for your financial well-being. However, that doesn't mean that you have to do everything yourself. There's no reason why you shouldn't hire a financial advisor, such as a financial planner, tax attorney, or stockbroker, to advise you about financial decisions. However, if you hire an expert, remember that the ultimate financial responsibility and decision making still lie with you.

There are several advantages to having a financial expert advise you. One is that this is the expert's full-time job. That alone is a significant benefit, because the expert closely monitors what is going on in the financial world. Financial planners and other experts have emerged in the last three decades to help consumers wade through the variety and complexity of investments. An expert understands the products and has the experience of working with other investors. He or she can quickly narrow down the best possibilities for you to focus on.

If you decide to hire an expert, make certain that you choose someone who you trust. Ask your friends and business contacts for referrals. You will probably want to meet with at least three or four people and discuss how they work with clients, their approach to creating a financial plan, and your expectations.

During this time, you also will want to discuss the person's experience and qualifications. For instance, if this person is a financial planner, does he or she use the certified financial planner (CFA) designation? If this person is selling products, does he or she have the necessary federal securities licenses, such as the National Association of Securities Dealers' Series 7 (to sell general securities), Series 6 (to sell mutual funds), and Series 63 (state licensing exam)?

While you can use the advice of an expert, it is up to you to evaluate that advice and make your own decisions. Make certain that you stay actively involved in your finances. While it may be tempting to trust someone to look out for your best interests, the truth is that the only person who will do that is you. If you are monitoring your investments and using the advice of a professional, you will be able to enjoy the best of both worlds.

28.

Economics Made Simple

The term "economics" may stop some people cold, because they view economics as a complex topic that requires a Ph.D. to understand. Nothing could be further from the truth, if you simplify it enough. By taking a little time to gain a basic understanding of even the most complex topic, you will soon be on your way to mastering it. Have faith in yourself to learn what you need to understand.

The performance of the economy is tracked by economic statistics that are released monthly by the U.S. government. Paying attention to a few key statistics can greatly enhance your understanding of economics.

One of the best well-known economic statistics is the unemployment report released on the first Friday of the month by the U.S. Labor Department. Obviously, if the number of people who are working increases, that is a good situation. The unemployment report is probably the single most important report that is released each month, because the number of people working has an overwhelming bearing on the economic health of a country.

Another important determinant of a country's economic health is consumer activity. This typically is charted in retail sales figures that are released monthly by the U.S. Department of Commerce. Retail sales figures show consumers' spending levels in the United States, which actually dwarfs expenditures made by businesses. Consumers create about two-thirds of the gross domestic activity, thanks to the proliferation of credit cards, a decade of relatively low unemployment, and mortgage interest rates at historic lows that have allowed consumers to borrow funds on the equity in their homes and spend the money on purchases of goods and services.

Inflation statistics also are closely watched. If inflation heats up and rises above four percent, for example, that can be problematic for the economy. Prices that rise too fast erode the purchasing power of consumers, which reduces spending on goods and services. If inflation rises, businesses will be hurt, because the Federal Reserve will raise interest rates. That, in turn, will drive up interest rates that businesses have to pay on borrowed funds, which will lower their profits and possibly result in layoffs.

Economics can be simple. The key is to take a little time to understand a few basic concepts so that you can continue to add to your knowledge.

29.

Demystifying the DJIA

One good way for beginning investors to decrease their stress level quickly is to learn the basic definitions of investing terms and then build upon that knowledge. The Dow Jones Industrial Average (DJIA) is probably one of the most well-recognized stock market terms. However, few people understand what it means.

The DJIA includes thirty of the largest stocks that trade on the New York Stock Exchange (NYSE), representing a cross-section of industries. Often, the companies in the DJIA are referred to as blue-chip companies because of their stability, longevity, and ability to generate solid financial results. Because of their large size, if one company in the DJIA reports negative news, it will drag the other companies down with it, most likely resulting in a down day for the market.

The list of companies that make up the DJIA changes over time. Companies are removed from the list if their fortunes wane and are replaced by up-and-coming companies. However, you don't have to memorize the current members of the DJIA. The names of the thirty companies are printed each day in the *Wall Street Journal*, which is owned by Dow Jones, Inc.

To fully understand the DJIA, it is helpful to have a historical perspective. The forerunner of today's DJIA began on July 3, 1884, when Charles H. Dow, the founder of Dow Jones, Inc., created his Dow Jones Industrial Average. He saw that there was a need for a market indicator that would document trends and show what the overall market was doing. To create such an indicator, he chose the average closing prices of eleven stocks that he selected because they were actively traded shares of major companies.

Just by having a little information, you can demystify financial terms and concepts and reduce your stress level, because you no longer are hearing things that you don't understand. Your financial life will be under control.

30.

Check Out a Credit Union

Credit unions no longer are exclusively for teachers, union members, or employees of large companies. Now more than ever, many credit unions are opening their membership to non-employees or to those people who are in some way connected with the credit union's geographic area. That is good news for investors and consumers looking to maximize what they earn on interest, as well as reduce their borrowing costs.

Many credit unions offer savings accounts and certificates of deposit (CDs) that pay higher interest rates than comparable accounts at banks or savings and loans. Credit unions may pay half a percentage point more. For investors who are trying to do everything possible to maximize their returns, opening a credit union account is one way to accomplish that goal.

Credit unions are able to pay higher interest because they are cooperative businesses run for the benefit of their members. Because a credit union is a nonprofit institution, often costs are lower than comparable costs for a commercial institution. Because credit unions are owned by their members and not by shareholders, there are no dividends to be paid. Instead, the credit union can take that money and give it back to its members in the form of higher interest rates paid on deposits or lower interest charges on loans. Members also may pay less on loans than they would with commercial banks. Those loans can be used to pay for a car, boat, or other large purchases.

The next time that you are looking to take out a car loan or reinvest money from a maturing CD, consider opening a credit union account. A few calls to credit unions in your area or a search on the Internet may turn up credit unions that you would be able to join. Professional associations, such as the National Credit Union Association, may be able to provide referrals.

Few people have enough money that they can justify paying above market interest rates on loans or avoid earning the maximum amount of interest possible. Make sure that you are not cheating yourself, and check into what a credit union can offer you.

31.

Daily Finances in Five Minutes a Day

While it is easy to figure out how much you pay in rent and car payments, it is much more difficult to tabulate cash expenditures. While those may only be a few dollars a day, those expenses add up over time and can doom even the best-thought-out budget.

However, there's a painless way to figure out what you actually spend, and it doesn't take any longer than five minutes a day. Carry around a piece of paper in your wallet or a notepad, and write down what you spend during the day. At the end of the day, you can total up the expenses and see exactly what you have spent. If you do this each day for a week, you will have a good estimate of what you spend and be in a position to develop a realistic budget.

It can be quite tedious to track expenses, especially little cash expenditures. While most people don't want to keep track of their receipts for cash expenses such as the bus, lunch, or other incidental expenses, try doing this for just one day to see how relatively painless it can be.

Those expenses may be small, but they are important. While you may dismiss your lunch or soda as inconsequential, those expenses add up to a relatively large amount over a month. For example, seven dollars spent on lunch and a drink each of the twenty working days a month adds up to $140 that month.

Once you know what you spend each day, you are on your way toward putting yourself on a firm financial footing. If you have significant financial goals, such as purchasing a house, building a retirement nest egg, or paying off credit cards, knowing what you spend is the first step to accomplishing those longer-term goals.

Whatever you do, don't get discouraged. Taking one constructive action to improve your finances is better than having great goals and doing nothing. If you can spend five minutes a day to move closer to achieving your financial goals, isn't it worth the time?

32.

Find the Right Mutual Fund for You

During the last two decades, thousands of new mutual funds have sprung up, as Americans increasingly have become enthusiastic investors. Now, more than half of U.S. citizens own mutual fund shares. With all of these options, it is more important than ever to be smart when it comes to choosing funds in which to invest.

One of the best things that you can do is use the power of the Internet to help you with your research. Brokerage firms or investment advisory web sites often have tools to help you narrow down potential mutual funds that can save you time. You can search for funds based on their return over numerous periods, such as the current month, a one-, five-, or ten-year period, or over the life of the fund. You can also search for a mutual fund based on its fees. Major newspapers, especially business papers, also rank the results of mutual funds at the end of each quarter.

However, before you check the search engine or newspaper pullout section, do some preparatory work. One of the first things is to determine whether you are looking for a stock or bond fund. There are a variety of different funds within those categories. A bond fund may invest only in short- or long-term securities, or it may invest in all different types of bonds. A stock fund, however, may invest in relatively small companies, called small-cap, or large companies, called large-cap.

Another distinction for a stock mutual fund is whether it invests in a growth stock, which probably won't pay dividends though its stock price is expected to appreciate, or a value stock, which does pay a steady dividend but has slowed growth. You'll need to decide which investment strategy meets your needs. If you typically shy away from risk, then you probably will want a value fund.

When it comes to making smart investments, the key is to have the right information at your fingertips. Use the power of the Internet, as well as printed rankings, to make the right move and secure your financial future.

33.

Saving Money When
You Don't Have Any

Saving money doesn't have to be an overwhelming task, nor do you need a bigger paycheck before you can begin. Despite what you might think, you can save money even if you don't have a lot of extra cash. After all, who really has extra money? The key to saving is to begin, and then you can easily make small efforts that will produce large benefits. Here are five easy ways to begin saving money that will be painless but deliver results.

At the end of the day, collect your change and put it in a jar or other container. You won't miss those pennies, nickels, dimes, and quarters. While this may seem like a naïve idea, the change will add up quickly over a week's time. Add several weeks and months, and you'll have a reasonable amount of money.

Reduce your expenditures. Begin doing that by clipping coupons for products that you will buy.

Begin taking your lunch to work one or more days a week. The average lunch costs seven dollars. While that may not sound like a lot of money, by the end of the month you will have twenty-eight extra dollars. By the end of one year, you could have $336 saved. If you take your lunch twice a week, you will have $672 by the end of the year.

Don't spend your tax refund. Instead, put it directly into your savings account. What better way to boost your savings than by depositing your tax refund?

If you are feeling confident of your ability to save money, here's a tactic for people who are paid biweekly. Those people receive twenty-six checks during the year, resulting in two months with an additional paycheck. Deposit those two paychecks directly into your savings account.

The key to saving money isn't about focusing on what you can't do. Instead, it is focusing on what you can do. Don't focus on how inadequate your financial resources are. Even if the only thing that you can accomplish is saving your change, begin by doing that, and congratulate yourself for taking the first step toward creating a solid financial future.

34.

Do You Have Too Much Debt?

Opinions about debt vary. Some people believe that they shouldn't have any other debt than a mortgage and perhaps a car loan. Others feel that it doesn't matter if they typically have a $10,000 credit card balance. Who is right?

The answer is based on individual values and decisions. However, there are a few points to consider if you are wondering whether you might fit into the too-much-debt category.

First, if you can only pay the minimum amount due on your credit card or slightly more, you might be carrying too much debt. Anything else would mean that you are cutting into the money that you need to use to pay for rent, utilities, and groceries.

Another tell-tale sign that you have too much debt is when you've reached the credit card limit on several cards and are applying for new cards in order to continue spending. Or perhaps you are applying for new cards in order to pay one card by transferring the balance to your new cards.

Another indication that you have overextended yourself is if you receive calls from companies about late bill payments or from collection agencies. Another may be credit card companies that change the terms of your credit cards, either cutting your credit limits or raising the interest rates that you are charged.

Are your bills constantly on your mind? Do you keep coming up with plans to reduce your credit card debt but have a difficult time implementing them? If so, this is a strong indication that you may be carrying too much debt.

Finally, you probably have too much debt if you would be in an immediate financial bind if you lost your job. High debt payments increase the amount of money that you have to spend each month. By reducing your debt, you lower the amount of money that you would have to replace each month if you lost your job.

If you think that some of these situations sound familiar, stop and consider whether you have too much debt. If you conclude that you do, acknowledge yourself for coming to terms with a very difficult problem and then figure out how you will resolve the problem. Remember, the first step to solving the problem is recognizing that one exists.

35.

Let Charitable Giving Enrich Your Life

Most people assume that donating money or goods to a charity is something that they can do that will enrich the lives of other people. However, sharing some of your wealth, or even your modest resources with others, can enrich your life, as well.

Even if you aren't wealthy, donating a modest amount of money to a worthy cause—whether it is a food pantry, a homeless shelter, or an organization that is attempting to find a cure for an illness—is one way that you can realize just how much you really have. You don't have to give hundreds of dollars, either. Even if all you can give is ten or twenty dollars, that is better than nothing.

Charitable giving also allows you to enrich your children's lives and teach them valuable lessons. Take the time and effort to teach them at an early age that it is better to give than receive. Show them how rewarding it is to help people in need. Even if your family isn't wealthy, let them absorb the lesson that you have enough money to be able to share with others. With that in mind, hopefully they won't be jealous of others during their teenage and adult years when they encounter people who are much more wealthy than they are.

Actions are as important as donating money. Let your children select some of their toys or clothes that they have outgrown that remain in good shape and donate them to a children's shelter or other charity. You can take this one step further and encourage them to give away one or two toys that they receive at holidays or their birthdays to children who are less fortunate.

You also may work on a charitable project, such as fixing up housing for poor people, helping to repair or clean a shelter, or working in a food pantry. Even if you don't have extra cash to share, you can share your time and talents to enrich the lives of the people that you are helping and your own life at the same time.

36.

Create a Fresh Start After Bankruptcy

Financial problems can be as stressful as the death of a close friend or family member, severe health problems, or divorce. One of the worst financial problems is filing for bankruptcy. However, once you've made the hard decision that you can't pay back all of your creditors, there is no point in being depressed about the situation.

The founders of the United States believed that debtors' prisons were abhorrent and prohibited their existence. If the founding fathers had the foresight to forgive debtors, don't you think that you should forgive yourself? After all, the purpose of the U.S. bankruptcy system is to get rid of debt, not to continue punishing people who have made a mistake. You've been given a fresh start. If the government has said that there is no point in locking up debtors in prison, why should you put yourself in your self-imposed debtors' prison? Don't continue punishing yourself when, legally, you and your debt have been forgiven.

If you have filed for bankruptcy, what you need to realize is that you made a mistake. You spent more than you could afford, and the bills piled up. After going through the bankruptcy process, those debts are either wiped out or drastically reduced so that you'll pay back what you need to and get on with your life.

Remember, you don't get off easy in a bankruptcy proceeding. It can be intrusive, humiliating, and embarrassing. When you get a fresh start, you can apply what you've learned to your financial actions in the future and not repeat your mistakes.

Sometimes, people who implement many of the right financial strategies still end up in financial trouble, because they lost jobs during a bad period of unemployment, had a medical problem that made working impossible, or suffered from the spending actions of a spouse in a collapsing marriage. In that case, don't punish yourself. You did everything that you could to possibly make the right financial decisions, but circumstances conspired against you.

The purpose of bankruptcy is to give debtors a clean slate and allow them to get on with their life. Take that opportunity, and resolve not to get into the same situation twice.

37.

Four Steps to Setting Financial Goals

We've all heard how important it is to have financial goals, but sometimes it can be difficult to achieve those goals. Fortunately, there is a simple method that you can use to establish your financial goals and put yourself on the path to a firm financial footing.

The first thing to do is to determine what your most important financial goals are—buying a house, putting more money away consistently for retirement, or paying off debt. Once you have your possible options, evaluate what goals are most important to you or determine which one requires immediate action. Having one or two clearly developed goals that you firmly work toward is much better than having a handful of goals that you halfheartedly try to achieve.

Next, determine how you are going to implement your goals. Construct a simple but clear plan for implementation so that you know exactly what you need to do. Confusion is one excuse that people use to avoid difficult tasks. Don't let your own confusion get in the way of reaching your goal.

It is crucial that you give yourself a deadline. Without a deadline, your goal may exist as a good idea that you will get around to implementing one of these days. Even though no one likes deadlines, they help keep us honest.

The final step is to make a firm commitment to accomplish your stated goals. Without commitment, you may abandon your goals when things become difficult. In order to reinforce your commitment, write down your goals and put them someplace where you will see them each day—the bathroom mirror, for example. By frequently reading your goals, you will reinforce them in your mind. The more frequently you think about them, the more able your brain is to perceive that they can become a reality.

In order to bolster your commitment, tell a partner or close friend about your goals and your deadlines. Ask him or her to check with you periodically to make certain that you are progressing. While we sometimes are quick to give up the battle by ourselves, if there is the chance that we will be embarrassed in front of other people, human nature often pushes us to go the extra mile. That just may be the secret to successfully implementing your goals.

38.

Four Ways to Win with Stocks

The stock market may have its ups and downs, but over the long term, stocks can provide solid returns to your portfolio. While it is important to understand how stocks can make you money, it is also important to realize that owning stocks doesn't guarantee that you will make money. If you have to sell at a time when the stock market, or your particular stock, is down, you could end up losing a significant amount of money.

One of the biggest advantages of stocks is that they can appreciate in value. If you start out with a stock that you purchased for twenty dollars, it may be as high as forty dollars within a matter of months. The stock may grow based on a sharp rise in the stock market, or it may trade higher because of specific news that applies to its company. For example, the share price of a pharmaceutical company may soar if the company receives approval from the Food and Drug Administration for a new drug. Alternatively, if a company does a really good job of beating its earnings estimates or taking away market share from its competitors, its share price will soar, too.

Additionally, many stocks pay a quarterly dividend, which returns some of the money that the company made to its owners, or shareholders. For the investor who wants investments to generate income, stocks may fill this need.

Stocks also avoid the ravages of inflation. Over time, money invested in the stock market will appreciate at a rate that typically exceeds the rate of inflation. In contrast, an investment such as a savings account or CD will not appreciate in value beyond the interest that it earns. If inflation occurs, the value of that CD will be eroded.

Finally, stocks are tax-efficient investments. If the share price appreciates and you sell the shares, you will pay taxes on the profit based on the capital gains tax rate, which typically is lower than your individual income tax rate.

In order to be an informed and relaxed investor, it is important that you understand the benefits of owning stocks, as well as the potential problems. If you have the right information, you can make the right decision.

39.

Frugality Is Your Friend

The twenty-first century has ushered in lower stock markets, higher unemployment, and general economic uncertainty. Not surprisingly, frugality is in, and designer brand products have lost a significant amount of their luster.

Rather than feeling as if you are depriving yourself, make frugality a game. Try to find out just how little you can spend and see what deals you can find. You might even enjoy it. For instance, discover new parts of town and new restaurants that are off the beaten track. You are likely to find excellent meals for as little as half the price of other, more mainstream restaurants. You also will be discovering new territory, which can be quite fun.

If you want to travel, one of the easiest ways to search out deals on hotels and airfare is to look at travel sites on the Internet. For procrastinators, this is a wonderful way to book a vacation. If you are looking for a short trip for the upcoming weekend, there are many last-minute deals available.

Another area where significant savings can be made is clothing purchases. Instead of buying an outfit the first time that you see it, wait until it goes on sale. Not many weeks will pass before you see a thirty- or forty-percent-off sign. Also explore shopping at discount department stores, which have increased the quality and appeal of their clothes.

For the person who really is into a bargain-hunting adventure, explore resale shops or garage sales. You often can purchase goods at extremely low prices and have a good time in the process.

You probably don't want to purchase an electronic item, such as a stereo or television, used. Conduct your own research on the Internet. Within a few hours, you can locate the lowest price possible.

Spending less money doesn't have to be about depriving yourself. Instead, turn it into your own version of a treasure hunt, and enjoy your pleasantly earned savings.

40.

Value Is In

During the stock market and Internet boom of the late 1990s, it seemed as though everyone was becoming a millionaire overnight. The boom was followed by a stock market that could go in no direction but down. Thanks to the bubble bursting, people's expectations have come back to earth. The rule of the day is that value once again is king. While this might not be glamorous, it does represent a return to reality. In the long run, that isn't a bad thing.

Nowhere has the concept of value been more important than the stock market. No longer are stock prices expected to double, especially when the company has only lost money. As a result, investors are beginning to buy stocks that are reasonably priced in companies which create products that people currently need.

Because you aren't able to double your money through stock market gains or super-sized bonuses, a different tactic is needed. A regular savings plan where a set amount of money is set aside each month now has come back into fashion. Instead of waiting for the home run equivalent of a large bonus, take some easy actions each month to set aside money that is available for emergencies or to create wealth. While everyone used to save money on a regular basis, that strategy soon fell out of favor as stock options and bonuses took over. As people return to the concept of value, they are returning to regular savings plans as well.

Value also is helping to bring reason to the housing market, which in many areas saw the value of homes and apartments skyrocket. Buying a house or apartment is typically the largest expenditure most Americans will make in their lifetime. With value coming back into the market, the instances of bidding against someone for a property have diminished drastically.

For those people who didn't fully catch the wave of the stock market and Internet boom, the return of value into the market will appear to be a breath of fresh air. Once again, common tasks available to everyone, such as saving money and purchasing value stocks, are back in vogue.

41.

Give Up Credit Cards for a Month

Are you frustrated by your inability to save money and achieve your financial goals because your credit card bills are piling up? Is the stress ruining your life and causing arguments in your household?

If this sounds familiar, take a minute to evaluate what is really important in your life. If your credit cards are making your life miserable, ask yourself just how necessary those credit card purchases are. You work hard and spend long hours earning your paycheck. Why shouldn't you have the money available to achieve your goals and take care of yourself and your family?

The solution is simple. Quit using your credit cards—just for one month. You might be pleasantly surprised how easy it is to pay cash or write checks for purchases. If you can't possibly manage without plastic (to buy an airplane ticket, for example) use a debit card.

By resolving not to use your credit cards for one month, you'll realize that you can leave them at home for a longer period of time.

Don't think about that yet, however. You don't have to go cold turkey all at once and create more anxiety. All you have to do is focus on one month. If you want to pay off your credit cards, what better way to start than by not adding additional charges for a month?

Create a new habit for yourself by not using your credit cards. After all, if you get used to the idea of putting cash down for drinks after work, or writing a check for department store purchases, that is a very potent way for you to see that you are spending "real" money, not just charging something.

It is never easy to get spending under control. There are thousands of enticing ways to use your money. Make it easy on yourself and take on one small project to reduce your expenditures. If you do that, you will be on your way to taking control of your finances and creating peace and harmony in your household.

42.

Get a Free Newspaper Subscription

Throughout the week, your newspaper is filled with a variety of coupons that can save you money on a variety of purchases. By clipping coupons, you can save enough money to pay for your newspaper subscription. For instance, if your newspaper costs around thirty dollars a month for home delivery, you would need to find a coupon or coupons that will save you about a dollar a day in order to pay for the subscription.

The Sunday paper will have several dozen pages of coupons that take anywhere from twenty-five cents to several dollars off products, especially in the case of multiple purchases. By clipping those coupons and using them to purchase the products that you need, you can rack up the savings.

However, clipping grocery coupons may be a bit tedious, especially if you don't do much grocery shopping. Instead, you may want to focus your efforts on the coupons that will save you a significant amount of money in one purchase.

Retail stores frequently offer coupons. Retail coupons have grown in popularity during the past few years as retail stores attempt to boost low sales. Stores often will place coupons in the advertisements that give ten, twenty-five, or even forty percent off your entire purchase for a certain period of time. While they have restrictions, these coupons may be applied to clothing, shoes, home furnishings, tools, or sporting goods. If you save twenty percent on a $400 purchase, that amounts to eighty dollars, which pays for nearly three months of your newspaper subscription. A more expensive purchase may result in your entire year's subscription being paid.

Very few people, including the rich, have as much money as they want. The key to improving your financial situation is to do as much as you can to maximize the money that you have. If that means clipping coupons to fully pay for one of your monthly expenses, then it may be worth embracing this option. After all, it's your money. Why not make it go as far as possible?

43.

Help Others While Saving Money

Most of us want to take actions that will help other people whenever possible. One way we can do that is to share some of our money with others who are less fortunate. By helping others, you can end up reducing the amount of income tax that you have to pay.

Instead of throwing away the letters from charitable organizations that request donations, begin reading them and consider sending in a donation. The amount doesn't have to be large. Money for a charitable organization can be deducted from your income tax, which will save you money. With one check, you have effectively fulfilled two purposes: saving money and helping other people.

You may have a favorite charity, your church, or a nonprofit group that is involved in a social issue such as animal welfare to which you can donate. In that case, your decision about where to send money is much easier, because you know which organization you strongly back. Then it is a matter of deciding how much you can donate.

By focusing your major donation activity at one source, you'll obtain several benefits. If your employer matches employees' charitable donations, then your $500 or $1,000 can go a lot further than your donation alone. Also, organizations typically offer benefits to their donors as an incentive to make them donate more money. A museum or theater may offer large donors free or discounted tickets to events or may invite them to special receptions held before or after performances. In addition to supporting a cause that you value, you'll also be able to invite a friend along to a nice event for less than you otherwise would have had to pay.

It is a pleasant experience to do what you can to help other people. However, there is no reason why you can't help yourself in the process. A win-win situation is good for everyone, and charitable donations create that situation.

44.

Hire a Realtor

A house typically will be the most important and most expensive purchase that a person ever makes in his or her lifetime. A realtor can help you with all aspects of buying a home. A realtor that you hire works for you instead of working for the seller, giving you an informed and educated ally on your side.

The first thing that a realtor can do is help you focus on areas that might be undervalued or help you narrow down the areas where you are looking. Realtors also have their own network to find out about houses that are soon going on the market, which may give you an advantage over other potential buyers.

Once you decide on a property to buy, the realtor can help you construct an offer that is competitive but as low as possible. If you are in a situation where there are competing bids, a realtor will be invaluable. Then, when you strike a deal with the seller, your realtor can guide you through the maze of financing and the closing process, thereby reducing your stress considerably.

45.

Do Financial Planners Work for Free?

Financial planners offer valuable services to millions of investors. To fully benefit from their assistance, you should understand how they are paid and where the fees are located. After all, you will be paying the bill.

Many financial planners work on a commission-only basis. This means that when you decide to purchase a life or disability insurance product or a stock or mutual fund, the planner will earn a commission on that product. So if you invest $1,000 in a mutual fund that has a load, or a sales charge, of four percent, only $960 of that money will be invested in the fund. The financial planner will receive forty dollars.

Do you want to pay that money? If the financial planner has reviewed your financial goals, listened to what is important to you, and recommended investments that fit those needs, it can be money well spent. This can be a tricky situation, because the commission may not obvious. If you work with a financial planner on a commission-only basis, make certain that you are fully informed about the fees, so you can make the right choice for your circumstances.

In contrast, another way that financial planners make money is by charging fees that are very obvious, such as an hourly rate that ranges from $100 to $350 per hour, or a flat fee to prepare a financial plan, which may range from $1,500 to over $5,000. Which fee structure is better? That's for you to decide. Some people feel more secure paying a flat fee or hourly rate, because they believe that they will get advice untainted by the planner's desire to earn the largest commission possible. If someone is working on a commission-only basis, what is to prevent them from recommending investments that have the highest commission but not necessarily the highest benefit for the investor?

Another fee combination involves charging a fee for the financial planning work plus commissions on any investments that are made. This puts financial planners in the best position to earn the most money.

As an investor, you need to be fully informed about fees so that you can make an educated decision about what situation is right for you. Make certain that you assert your rights and find out all of the details.

46.

Your Social Security

During the last several years, the Social Security Administration has made it easier to monitor what retirement benefits you are likely to receive. The Social Security Administration is required by law to send annual statements to workers age twenty-five and older who have paid Social Security taxes through their job or self-employment who currently aren't receiving benefits. The statements are sent out about three months before each worker's birthday.

However, those statements are only useful if Social Security has your correct mailing address, so naturally, verifying this information is your first step. This can be done by calling Social Security or by transmitting this information on its web site.

If you haven't received a statement yet and you fit the above criteria, apply online to receive it. You will need to provide your name as it appears on your Social Security card, your Social Security number, your date and place of birth, and your mother's maiden name, which helps identify you.

The Social Security statement includes a record of your earnings that have had Social Security taxes deducted. It also includes an estimate of the benefits that you and your family are likely to receive. The calculations are made for three retirement ages: sixty-two, sixty-seven, and seventy. Additionally, the statement will tell you what disability payments you are eligible for and will indicate whether you have earned enough to qualify for Medicare.

It is important to review the statement closely. You'll want to make certain that there are no mistakes on your record. If there are, resolving them sooner and closer to the time that they occurred is much easier than trying to do this at age sixty, as you are preparing for retirement. After all, who is likely to have kept pay stubs or tax records that would prove what you earned from a job that you held thirty years earlier?

The other important reason for obtaining this information is that you can calculate how much money you will need for retirement. Use that information to empower yourself to begin planning for retirement now—you can reduce your stress level and know that you are prepared.

47.

How the Federal Reserve Helps You

When most people think about the Federal Reserve, they think about interest rates. About every six weeks, the Fed's Federal Open Market Committee (FOMC) meets to discuss interest rate policy. The FOMC may raise short-term interest rates, lower them, or leave them alone. The Fed can change its federal funds rate, which is the interest rate that one bank will loan another bank overnight. If the Fed decreases its target for the federal funds rate, it has essentially lowered interest rates, and other interest rates will move lower, as well. Lower interest rates stimulate economic activity by making borrowed money less expensive, prompting businesses and individuals to borrow more.

However, if interest rates move too low and cause frantic borrowing and business activity, then inflation can emerge. A steady, moderate level of inflation, such as two to three percent, is a good thing, while inflation above that level for a sustained period of time causes problems. With high inflation, consumers feel as though their paychecks aren't keeping up with rising prices, and they are losing economically. For people on fixed incomes, such as retirees, inflation can be a serious problem.

The Fed works carefully to make certain inflation doesn't get out of control. Thus, if it appears that inflation is rising, the Fed will raise interest rates. Higher interest rates increase the cost of doing business and will slow down business activity, which will restrain inflation.

The Fed also supervises and regulates banks that are federally chartered. Of particular concern to the Fed is that consumers are treated fairly by banks, especially in making sure that both federal- and state-chartered banks don't employ discriminatory lending practices. Banks are closely monitored by the Fed, which conducts a quarterly survey of banks' credit practices to gauge lending activity and the strength of the economy.

It isn't necessary to become an expert on the workings of the Federal Reserve. However, by understanding what the Fed does, you can greatly increase your financial knowledge and do a better job of taking care of your money.

48.

Inflation Is Your Friend

Throughout much of the 1970s and into the 1980s, inflation was a serious economic problem. Rising price levels eroded individuals' and businesses' purchasing power, which made it seem that everyone was falling behind economically, even though they were working harder.

However, by the spring of 2003, the situation had changed, and Federal Reserve policy makers were worrying about deflation, or falling prices. Deflation hurts the economy, because falling prices may lead to decreasing wages and layoffs, which makes it that much harder for people to pay back their debts. More defaults produce more economic problems. Lower wages lead to less consumer spending, which then causes another round of lower economic activity.

Neither extreme is good. Instead, what is best is a moderate level of inflation, such as two to three percent. For much of the 1990s and into the 2000s, inflation tricked along at a moderate pace that allowed prices to rise slightly but didn't erode purchasing power.

If inflation dips below one percent, then the Fed begins to worry about deflation, which potentially can be much more damaging to an economy than inflation. That possibility came to light in May 2003. Fed chairman Alan Greenspan said that while the risk of deflation was small, it was worth making sure that it didn't materialize.

Typically, the Fed cuts interest rates to stimulate the economy. Lower interest rates make it cheaper to borrow money for both businesses and consumers. The lower prices encourage borrowing, which stimulates the economy. However, the Fed found itself in a bind when its key short-term interest rate, the Fed funds rate, declined to 1.00 percent in June 2003—the lowest it had been since 1958. Interest rates can't fall below zero, which means that the Fed may be running out of ammunition to stimulate the economy. Interest rates closer to zero also pose problems for money market mutual funds, which might not be able to earn enough money to provide investors with a return and cover their expenses.

So the next time you complain about rising prices, just remember: a moderate level of inflation is beneficial to the economy. Otherwise, you have deflation, which brings its own set of economic problems.

49.

Avoiding Debt Is the Key to Feeling Better

Nothing is worse than working hard but feeling as though you are digging yourself into a deeper and deeper financial hole. That is exactly what happens when you let credit card balances mount. The effect of compounded interest can destroy even the most valiant attempts to pay off your credit card balance.

To prevent this from happening, don't let the balances build in the first place. By letting your debt build, you will be upset each month when the credit card bill arrives in the mail. Don't put yourself in a position of dreading to open the mail every day. Instead, feel better and avoid debt.

Before charging something, think ahead thirty days and envision just how important that restaurant meal or clothing purchase will be. The value will probably pale in comparison to your other financial goals, such as buying a house or funding your retirement. Don't make yourself feel bad by not being able to reach your goals. Instead, make yourself feel better by not accumulating debt and avoiding the future stress that will be a part of that debt.

50.
Invest in Land

"Land is the only thing in the world worth working for, worth fighting for, worth dying for; because it's the only thing that lasts," said Scarlett O'Hara's father in the award-winning novel and movie, *Gone with the Wind*. It is a refrain that has hit home with many people who want to make sure that their next investment isn't going to suffer the same fate as their once-hot telecom stocks or shares in initial public offerings (IPOs).

As a result, many individuals have decided to invest their money in real estate, either by improving their current homes or buying vacation properties that can be used personally or rented out as an investment property. With all of this recent interest in real estate, land prices have mostly continued to hold their value, even though the number of people without jobs has risen since the stock market peaked in 2000.

Thus, many people feel much more comfortable investing their assets in land now, especially in contrast to stocks, bonds, or other types of assets. This isn't surprising—land and home prices mostly have made steady increases since the end of World War II.

However, just because you invest your money in real estate doesn't mean that it is a sure thing. For instance, all markets are cyclical, and the real estate market is no exception. If you end up having to sell your property at the wrong time in the cycle, you could lose money. There is also no guarantee on how much appreciation you will receive. What you thought might be a sure thing may turn out to provide only paltry returns.

If you decide to invest in a vacation property, you may have some additional risks beyond what you have investing in a house that you live in. For instance, if the vacation area decreases in popularity, you could lose money when you decide to sell your house. If you have purchased in a vacation area where there aren't many home or condo units, and five years later, it ends up overbuilt, you could lose money or not earn the return that you anticipated.

There are no surefire investments. However, land does offer one way for the long-term investor to earn a solid return.

51.

Investment Banking Made Easy

Investment banking refers to services that banks provide their corporate customers that they don't offer to retail customers. These services include helping companies raise capital by selling stocks or bonds and advising them about merging with other companies. In contrast, commercial banks provide money to companies by giving them loans.

During the technology boom of the late 1990s, almost everyone heard about IPOs. As you might expect, an IPO is the first time that a company sells shares, or equity, to the public. An IPO transforms a privately owned company into one that is owned by public shareholders. During the boom, a record number of companies went public, which propelled investment bankers into the limelight.

However, IPOs aren't the only way that companies raise money from equity offerings. When a company is already public, it can have a secondary stock offering, which also would be made by investment bankers. A secondary stock offering means that the company is selling additional shares of stock to the public. If a company is selling stock for the third or fourth time, the offering is still called a secondary or follow-on offering.

Investment bankers also are involved with helping companies raise money through debt offerings. Typically, corporations will issue notes and bonds and sell those to the public. Short-term debt also is sold, which includes commercial paper (270 days or less until maturity) or a revolving credit line, which must be renewed every year.

Another service that is provided by investment bankers is advice on mergers and acquisitions. If a company is contemplating acquiring another company, it will usually hire an investment bank to advise it on the transaction, including the price and the deal's structure. The investment bank also will negotiate with the target company. Similarly, if a company has received an offer to be bought out by another company, it will hire an investment bank to advise it on how to get the highest possible offer.

While investment banking may sound complicated, it doesn't have to be. By having a basic understanding of investment banking, you can put new information into an appropriate context and increase your knowledge.

52.

Use Automatic Bill Payment Services

Many banks offer online banking and telephone bill payment services that let you schedule when your bills should be paid. On the specified date, funds are withdrawn from your checking account; they are either electronically transmitted, or the bank mails a paper check.

This technique can help you save time. When you receive your bill, open it and make sure that it is accurate. Then turn on your computer and go to the bill payment services' web page. Enter the payee, the amount, and the day that it should be paid. For instance, if the electric bill is due on the eighteenth of the month, you can schedule it to be paid seven to ten days before the due date. Your bill will be paid on time. You also have eliminated one item from your to-do list and removed the danger that your bills will pile up and create a large weekend project for you when you would rather be having fun.

By selecting a payment date that is relatively close to the due date, you are maximizing the amount of interest that you earn on the money on deposit in your checking account. While the sum may not be huge, you deserve to earn every possible dollar that you can. If your checking account fees are assessed based on your balance, you will want to hold on to that money as long as possible.

If you don't have a computer, don't worry. The same outcome can be accomplished with telephone bill payment services offered by some banks. To set this up, you give the payment service a list of the bills that you pay each month, along with your account numbers and the addresses where the payments are mailed. To pay your bills, call a toll-free number; enter the number of the bill you are paying, the amount, and the day of the month that it should be paid. Within minutes, all of your bills will be paid, saving you the time and effort of writing checks, purchasing stamps, and mailing the bills.

While no one looks forward to paying bills, by using online or telephone bill payment services, you can minimize the pain of spending your hard-earned money. While those services won't make your bills go away, they will help you spend the least amount of time and effort to pay them.

53.

Try Dollar-Cost Averaging

Dollar-cost averaging is the system of buying stocks, mutual funds, or other investments on a regular basis, regardless of what direction prices are headed. The system gives investors the discipline to continue purchasing shares when prices are both low and high. For investors with a long-term horizon who believe that the returns will average out over time, dollar-cost averaging keeps them investing on a regular basis.

Here's how dollar-cost averaging works. The investor commits to investing the same amount of money each month. If share prices are low, then the money buys more shares, somewhat like shopping in a store that is having a sale. If prices are high, fewer shares are purchased. Thus, money is invested each month, regardless of what the market is doing.

The advantage of dollar-cost averaging is that you avoid the psychological reluctance to purchase shares when prices are falling. However, this is exactly when shares should be purchased, because they are essentially "on sale."

Dollar-cost averaging also keeps people in the market and avoids the tendency to want to "time" the market and wait for the bottom, which is very difficult to do. Instead, dollar-cost averaging spreads out your risk over time and ensures that all of your purchases aren't done at the top of the market.

While the dollar-cost averaging gives discipline to investors and can reduce risks, it doesn't eliminate risks. If you are buying shares through a dollar-cost averaging program during a sustained down market, which occurred for several years during the first years of the twenty-first century, you very well could end up with substantial losses, even over the long term.

However, by using dollar-cost averaging to invest in the market, you can smooth out the gains and losses, and over the long term, earn solid returns. At the very least, it instills discipline so that investors continue to stay in the market, rather than waiting for the perfect opportunity, which may not arrive.

54.

Government Money for Your House

The U.S. government wants you to own a home, and it is putting money in your pocket to help you achieve that goal. The government's help comes in the form of a tax break that gives taxpayers the ability to deduct the interest that they pay on the mortgage of their primary residence. This deduction, along with the appreciation in real estate, makes owning a home a very attractive proposition.

Here's how it works. The amount of interest that you pay on your mortgage for your principal residence is recorded on Schedule A, the IRS form that goes along with your 1040. The deductions on Schedule A are taken from your adjusted gross income on the first page of the 1040.

In short, if you have $75,000 in adjusted gross income, which is arrived at by subtracting eligible deductions such as moving expenses, alimony paid, and deductions for IRAs, you can deduct the amount of the mortgage interest paid from the amount of adjusted gross income, which lowers the amount of taxes that you have to pay. With $10,000 in mortgage interest, the amount of income that you would have to pay taxes on would be $65,000, not $75,000. A single person in the twenty-eight percent tax bracket would save $2,800 in taxes just from this one tax break.

If you take out a home equity line of credit to pay off bills, redecorate your house, or pay for a large purchase such as a vacation or new car, the interest charged on your home equity line of credit also is deductible. However, the home equity credit line and mortgage aren't the only mortgage-related expenses that can be deducted. Home buyers who have to pay points on a mortgage also may deduct the cost of those points in the year that they are paid, making the year that you purchase a home a particularly lucrative one for tax deductions. A point is a fee charged by a bank in return for granting a mortgage. One point equals one percent of the mortgage. One point on a $100,000 mortgage would cost $1,000.

For many people, building up equity in the home is one of the best ways to create wealth. Adding in a tax deduction makes it a particularly economical way to live, because typically, money will show up after you file your tax return. If the government is giving you money to own a house, why not take it?

55.

Car Shopping via Computer

The next time that you are in the market for a car, don't go any farther than your computer. Since car makers and third-party services discovered that the web makes a great selling platform, consumers have been handed a potent tool that makes buying a car easy. In fact, no more effort is involved than moving your fingers on the keyboard.

The Internet helps car buyers collect a large quantity of knowledge that will allow them to begin narrowing their choices. After you begin to identify some cars that you like better than others, there are hundreds of car reviews that can be read, with some web sites entirely devoted to reviews. You can browse pictures and descriptions of cars just as you would in a car lot.

Once you begin to look for a car, there are many web sites that sell cars. You can use these sites to undertake a substantial price comparison campaign. Why not check out prices from ten different dealers, especially if it doesn't involve driving from one auto lot to another?

After deciding what car you want, you will probably want to take it for a test drive. This is where your local car dealer will be helpful. The test drive also will provide you with an opportunity to obtain the best price possible from the car dealer, because you will begin the negotiating process armed with information. If it turns out that you can purchase the car for less on the Internet, you can take that route. However, if the car dealer offers you other enticements to purchase the car, then you have improved your original Internet deal.

When you arrive back home, you can return to the Internet and search for a car loan among dozens of lenders to see who will offer you the best interest rate. You can search for auto insurance, as well.

With no more than a few hours on the computer, you can explore numerous possibilities for purchasing your car at the best possible price. By shopping via computer, you've saved a great deal of money and made your life easier.

56.

Life Insurance

If you are responsible for your family's economic well-being, you have to plan ahead in the event of your untimely death. While there will be many considerations, one of the easiest things that you can do is to purchase life insurance. Even though life insurance won't eliminate the emotional strain and despair that your family will feel, it will prevent immediate financial problems.

First, you should determine how much insurance you need. Will your spouse need cash to pay off a mortgage? Perhaps you have a good bit of debt outstanding that is perfectly acceptable while your paycheck arrives each month. With your death, that paycheck would disappear, but your bills will remain.

Next, you have to determine whether you want term or permanent life insurance. There are advantages and disadvantages to each policy. Term life insurance insures you for a specific term— usually a year. As you get older, the amount of insurance increases each year, unless you have a policy that locks in the cost for a specific time period. This is the least expensive type of insurance, and may cost several hundred dollars for an adult in his or her thirties or forties.

Permanent life insurance insures you as long as you continue to pay your premiums. This type of life insurance and its variations—whole life, universal life, and variable life—provide an investment vehicle in addition to the death benefit. Over time, the cash value of the insurance plan will build. If you are in a financial bind, you may be able to borrow against the policy or use some of that cash value to pay your premium. However, the death benefit will be reduced by the amount of the loan outstanding.

Financial experts disagree on whether term or permanent life insurance is better. One school of thought says that you should buy term insurance and then invest the difference between the permanent policy premium, probably several thousand dollars annually, and the cost of the term insurance, which probably is several hundred dollars. You will earn a larger return from your own investment compared with the return that the insurance company will pay.

Life insurance gives your family breathing room to cope with the emotional upset of your death instead of instantly being worried about next month's bills. With that in mind, life insurance is an invaluable lifeboat.

57.

Make Your Money Work for You

In difficult economic times, a smart strategy is to maximize income while at the same time reducing expenses as much as possible. While checking accounts or CDs often don't pay high interest rates, there is no reason why you shouldn't maximize the amount of money that you earn on these types of accounts.

If you keep even an extra $500 or $1,000 in your checking account, it would pay you to look around for accounts that pay more interest. Alternately, you might find a checking account with significantly lower expenses. There are three primary areas to explore in order to maximize what you earn in interest from the funds on deposit in your checking account.

First, investigate financial firms that are likely to pay higher rates of interest, such as credit unions. Perhaps you know that there is a credit union associated with your company or profession. Teachers and federal government employees are two groups that typically have access to large credit unions. Go online or call the credit union to find out how much interest it pays on its checking and savings accounts and CDs. If the rate is more than your current accounts, then you should consider switching your accounts, or at least investing your next CD or savings account there.

Another type of business that pays attractive interest rates is an online bank. These banks have to pay more to attract customers, because people aren't as comfortable with online bank accounts as they are with banks whose premises they can walk into. Enter "online banking" into a search engine, and see what names appear. Then click on the link to a web page and find out how much interest that bank pays on checking and savings accounts, as well as CDs.

Finally, pay attention to the advertisements that the banks in your area are placing. Are you seeing the names of new banks? If so, these banks are probably attempting to grow and are trying to find new customers. The interest rate that the new competitors pay, or the lower fees that they charge, will benefit you.

While you won't get rich by switching your accounts to obtain higher interest, there is no point in turning away extra money. Don't you think it's about time that your money went to work along with you?

58.

Specific Financial Goals

If you decide to get your finances under control, trying to do too much at once can be as bad as doing nothing at all. Instead, having one specific goal can be much more effective than having a dozen goals that amount to nothing more than good intentions.

To avoid those good intentions, prioritize your goals. For instance, buying a house may be your most important goal. You can begin by finding out what house you can afford. Perhaps your investigation reveals that you don't have enough money to buy a house. However, now you understand how much money you will need to do so. You can create another goal to make a monthly savings program so that you will be able to meet your home ownership goal. Once you've purchased your home, you can begin prioritizing what you want to accomplish next, whether that is saving more for retirement or purchasing a new car.

When you prioritize, at the end of the day, you will have achieved one accomplishment and can relish that achievement. Then, bolstered by your success, you can move to the next goal.

59.

Painlessly File Your Income Taxes

No one looks forward to filing their income taxes, especially if they have to write a check to make up for an underpayment. Often, the stress of filing taxes begins when you attempt to locate the papers that you will need. This is one of the easiest problems to solve. In January, your employer will mail you a W-2 form that shows you how much money you made, less any 401(k) contributions, as well as the amount of federal, state, and local income tax withheld from your pay. Similarly, your bank and brokerage firm will mail you a 1099 form that shows how much in interest or dividends you earned.

When you receive the first form, designate one spot where you will put all of your future tax materials. This can be a file folder in a filing cabinet, a certain space in a drawer, or a file that sits on your desk. In order to avoid confusion, use a colored folder or write in big letters what the folder is.

Next, you need to obtain the income tax forms used for filing. There are several ways to do this, and here is where early preparation will make your life easier. In February or early March, go to your local library or post office to obtain the forms that you need. As a guide, review your taxes from last year to see what forms you used, because they probably will remain the same.

Another option is to download your forms from the IRS web page. During February or early March, few people are online downloading their forms. However, if you wait until late March or April, you may encounter a slower response from the Internet or even the inability to access the IRS web page, especially if you are trying during an evening or on the weekend.

By doing a little bit of preparatory work, you can approach your income taxes in the least stressful way possible. After all, you can't legally avoid paying income tax, but you do have total control of how you respond to the annual task. With that in mind, use a little organization to wipe away your stress.

60.

Paid Vacations

You can pay for your vacation without spending a dime, or a dollar, for that matter. It couldn't be easier.

First, figure out an amount of money that you wouldn't miss each month. Maybe that is $50, $100, or $200. Then set up a savings or money market account where you can automatically transfer that sum of money from your checking account every month. Because the amount is small by your standards, you won't even realize that the money has left your account.

When you plan your vacation, pay for the plane tickets, hotel room, meals, and car rental on one credit card. When the bill arrives, transfer money from your savings account into your checking account, and pay the balance on the credit card. Voilà—a free vacation that doesn't touch the funds in your checking account that you were earmarking to pay the rent and your other monthly bills! The charges won't remain on your credit card, either.

Because the money is in another account, you tend to forget about it and don't even think about spending it each month. In case you are tempted, the balance probably won't be large enough, at least in the early months, to make you think differently.

Your current bank or a new bank, such as an online bank that is paying higher interest rates in order to attract customers, is a good place to set up your savings account. Why not make your vacation fund grow faster by earning higher interest rates?

If fifty dollars a month isn't going to begin to pay for your vacation unless you wait several years, determine what your vacation is likely to cost, and divide that amount by the number of months that you have available to save. If you plan on taking one major vacation a year, then divide the cost of the vacation by twelve. That will tell you how much money you need to transfer each month to your new savings account.

By being able to pay your entire credit card balance a few weeks after returning from your vacation, you will be able to obtain peace of mind and avoid any guilty feelings about overspending on vacation. It may even feel like you've had an all-expenses-paid trip. What could be better than that?

61.

Plan for the Unexpected

It is impossible to know what difficulties life will throw your way. While money can't solve all of life's problems and it doesn't guarantee happiness, it can be powerful enough that some of your problems may seem easier to manage.

We all want to buy nice things and treat ourselves for working so hard. However, in the long run, saving a certain percentage of your salary very well may be the smartest financial move that you can make, and one that will add the most to your quality of life. Let your money provide you with the inner peace that comes with being able to overcome financial adversity.

One of the most common and stressful financial problems that people face is being laid off. However, if you have enough money saved, the financial stress can be lessened. Many financial planners recommend having about three to six months' living expenses on hand in the event that you lose your job. If you are laid off, typically you'll receive some severance pay, and you will be eligible for unemployment insurance. If you have six months of savings and those income streams, you have transformed a stressful event from a financial disaster into a situation that is manageable.

Other potential unexpected expenses include a broken heating or air conditioning unit or a roof that leaks. There is little discretion involved in whether those expenditures are made. They have to be, and that requires money. Your car may break down, requiring an expensive repair or purchasing a new one. Having some extra money tucked away lessens the irritation of having to spend the money and allows you to be prepared.

Having money available to pay for the unexpected good things in life is beneficial, as well. For instance, if a friend invites you to come on a week-long vacation to Hawaii or a hiking trip through the Appalachians, you don't want to be in a position of having to say no because you don't have enough money.

Make sure that you create the life that you want. Putting a little bit of money aside for a rainy day helps accomplish that goal.

62.

Procrastination Is a Big Expense

It's not surprising that people procrastinate about cutting expenses or saving for retirement. There are always unexpected expenses that occur during the month or recreation opportunities to spend money that you didn't anticipate. It's very tempting to put off fiscal responsibility for another month—but sometimes, that month turns into another month, and then a year. By putting off saving money, paying debts, and saving for retirement, you are in danger of accomplishing none of your financial goals. Each day that you wait makes the task that much more difficult.

For example, if you want to boost your investments and decide to purchase shares in a mutual fund for $2,000 in January, and then invest $100 a month for that year, if your fund earns eight percent a year, you will have $3,411. Now, if you delay your plans for six months and invest $2,000 in July and then $100 a month, at the end of that year, you will only have $2,691, assuming an eight percent rate of return. Just by delaying your plans for six months, you already are behind $720.

However, that pales in comparison to the impact that delaying contributions to your retirement will have on the availability of future funds. Assume that you put $2,000 a year, or $167 a month, into an IRA. If you continue to invest this money each month beginning at thirty, you will have $248,890 by the time that you are sixty and plan to retire. If you delay this plan until age forty, and invest until you are sixty, you will only have $98,366. That's a difference of $150,524 that you've missed out on by starting ten years later.

For anyone stymied by procrastination, here are several tips to get you started. First, pick one good idea to implement. It really doesn't matter what you choose. The important thing is that you are doing something. If being overwhelmed by options isn't your problem, then try telling a trusted friend what you plan to do and a date when you want to have accomplished this. Make a promise to both your friend and yourself that you will begin implementing your financial goal. Sometimes, it takes being embarrassed in front of friends to overcome procrastination. If that will motivate you, great! Begin eliminating the procrastination expense today.

63.

Disability Insurance

Disability insurance is one of the most expensive types of insurance, as well as the most valuable insurance policy, because it replaces some of your income if you become injured and are unable to work. For people who don't have an independent means of income or a large savings account, a solid disability policy is essential.

Depending on which set of statistics you look at, you'll see just how likely it is that you may become disabled. For instance, odds are 1 in 1,800 that you will have a fire, 1 in 70 that you will have an auto accident, and 1 in 18 that you will have a disability. While the individual odds may vary, you are much more likely to be disabled than to have your house burn down.

Even if you are convinced about the benefit of disability insurance, many people are stopped by the cost of the policy. Annual premiums may amount to one to three percent of your annual salary, which is a significant amount if you have to write out a monthly check. However, if you aren't covered by your employer's disability policy, you may want to carefully consider whether you can afford not to have disability insurance.

Other groups of people who especially should consider disability insurance are self-employed people and parents who stay home and take care of their children. Even though the stay-at-home parent isn't earning a paycheck, if he or she became disabled, money would be needed for tasks such as childcare, transportation, housecleaning, and cooking.

Before buying a policy, make certain that you understand all of its provisions. Most importantly, who determines if you are disabled? The insurance company or your doctor? What criteria are used to judge whether you are disabled? While it might seem straightforward now, if you do become disabled, you'll want to have thought through what criteria you are going to have to meet in order to obtain your benefits. You will also want to find out if the policy pays a partial benefit if you are partially disabled.

Disability insurance is probably one of the most important insurance policies that you can buy. Give it serious consideration when you are creating your financial plan.

64.

Protect Yourself with Savings

Even the most successful and highly paid person should have sufficient funds set aside for emergencies. You never know when you will need it.

How much is enough? It really depends what your circumstances are. Generally, three to six months of income is the suggested amount of money that should be set aside for unexpected events, such as the loss of a job. You'll need a sufficient amount of money on hand to give you some breathing room until you find another job.

While unemployment insurance will pay for some of your expenses, even the most generous states will pay no more than about $1,600 a month for people who have earned large salaries. For anyone paid on an hourly basis, unemployment is less than that.

Health problems can also create significant emotional stress on top of financial problems if you are underinsured or if your insurance company refuses to pay for a procedure you need. As companies increasingly attempt to reduce costs and insurance companies raise prices or reduce benefits, it makes it more likely that you are going to need to foot part of the bill.

Extra cash on hand is needed even if your health issue isn't life-threatening. For instance, if you want to obtain laser surgery to improve your eyesight, that typically won't be covered by your health insurance.

If you have children, you also need more money on hand. Children often have special needs that come with high price tags. For instance, your children may want dance or piano lessons or need extra help with schoolwork, which costs plenty. In order to provide for them, keep extra money on hand for those extras, not to mention emergencies.

Do yourself a favor and protect your financial well-being with sufficient savings. Hopefully, you won't have to use them, but if you do, they will be available.

65.

Buy a Bond

For most people, investing implies buying securities or stocks. Yet this can be one of the most volatile forms of investment. Stocks can yield high returns, but they can also result in huge losses. Loading a portfolio full of stocks is a mistake, because it lacks one very important element: diversification.

There's no better counterbalance to a falling equity market than bonds. Often, as the equity market falls, investors will shift some money into bonds, which drives down stock prices and pushes bond prices up.

Bonds also provide regular income through semiannual interest payments. While some stocks may pay dividends, that income isn't guaranteed. If a company has a bad year, it may decide to forego dividends. Bond issuers are compelled to pay interest, unless the bond is in default. However, that is an unlikely prospect if you've purchased high-quality bonds.

U.S. Treasury bonds or notes also offer the benefit of regular cash flow and the repayment of the principal upon maturity. Because

Treasuries are backed by the full faith and credit of the U.S. government, you can sleep soundly knowing that you aren't going to lose your money.

Another way to limit some of your risks is to invest in a bond mutual fund, which will own dozens of bonds. If one company does default on its bonds, it will hurt the bond fund's return, but it won't decimate your entire investment.

No investment is perfect, and bonds are no exception. If inflation rises, that will drive up interest rates. Your bonds will be worth less because they are paying interest rates that are now lower than current market rates.

Investors who are worried about inflation can purchase Treasury Inflation-Protected Securities (TIPS). Like other Treasury securities, they pay interest every six months. However, upon maturity, the principal that will be returned is indexed to inflation. Further, the interest payments are based upon the inflation-indexed principal amount, not the original amount. If inflation rises, so does the principal that you receive at maturity and in your regular interest payments. However, in the unlikely event that deflation occurs, TIPS guarantee that the minimum principal that will be returned is the bond's par value.

66.

Teach Your Children Financial Smarts

All parents want to teach their children as many lessons as possible, so that they will have healthy, happy, and secure lives. Some of the most important lessons to instill in children concern managing money.

These lessons have to be learned at home. Unlike mathematics, English, or science, there are no classes or degrees that can teach these lessons. If parents don't teach them, there is a strong chance that they won't be learned at all.

Make these lessons fun for your children. Take them to the bank and help them open up savings accounts. Explain how this works and help them with the multiplication so that they can see how interest is earned. Let them have the thrill and sense of accomplishment from putting some of their allowance or part-time income into their savings account. Encourage your children to set aside some of the money that they receive at holidays or birthdays into their savings accounts.

Even very young children can participate by putting money in a piggy bank. Let them go on a treasure hunt to collect change that they find around the house or in the car and deposit this money into their piggy bank. Let them "earn" a few dollars by doing tasks that are appropriate for their age. For instance, if you are doing lawn work, let your children earn a nickel for each dandelion or weed that they pick.

Allowances are a great way to teach older children about money. By making them spend their own money on their entertainment or other nonessential expenses, they will learn the value of money and how easily it can be spent. If they run out of money before their next allowance payment is due, they won't spend all of their money so quickly the next time. That simple lesson will provide many valuable returns after your children become adults and can't accelerate the arrival of their paychecks.

Don't shortchange your children by ignoring money and not teaching them the lessons that they need. Instead, instill in your children good financial values from an early age so that they will grow into financially savvy adults.

67.

Researching Investments with Ease

Thanks to the power of the Internet, you don't have to spend a lot of time or effort researching appropriate investments. For the investor who is just beginning the process of selecting investments, numerous investment web sites, such as those run by online brokerage firms, can provide you with some initial direction. For instance, these sites can help you determine whether you are a risk-averse investor or someone who is interested in taking on a decent amount of risk in order to increase your return. Web sites can also provide a wealth of information about how you should allocate your investments in your portfolio.

Once you've made a decision about what percentage of your portfolio should consist of stocks or bonds, you can narrow your options by using search engines on many online brokerage and investment web sites. These tools will help you consider different stocks within an industry by comparing revenues, price-to-earnings ratios, and a variety of other financial criteria. In the case of mutual funds, you can easily compare the returns of funds, along with minimum investments and associated fees. This will allow you to narrow your choices to a list of the five funds with the greatest returns and the lowest expenses.

When you have identified several companies or mutual funds that you may want to invest in, you will need to find out what each company has been doing in the last several months. Those same sites will probably provide a variety of articles written by media outlets or news releases from each company. Knowing whether a company is facing any increased competition, enforcement activity by the government, or declining sales is important before investing in any stocks, or even mutual funds.

Another benefit of using the Internet is that you can access research services provided by investment specialists. Web sites such as Morningstar.com provide a variety of information and advice for stock investors.

Thanks to the Internet, you can easily select appropriate investments. You can use the power of the Internet to bring the information to your fingertips as quickly and easily as possible.

68.

Revamp Your Social Life

Entertainment has become even more expensive than just a few years ago. Take matters into your own hands, and declare war against rising prices. Invite a few friends—or if you have the room, a dozen people—over for a night of home entertainment and conversation.

The quality of your life and the amount of fun that you have isn't measured in dollars. If you think back over some of the best times that you've had, they probably have been with close friends and likely didn't involve spending a lot of money. Instead, how much fun and enjoyment you have comes from spending time with your closest friends, not by the amount of money that you spend in one day or evening.

With this in mind, schedule a budget-conscious evening, and save money in the process. For instance, you can invite friends over and rent a movie or plan an event around a movie scheduled to air on a premium cable channel. After the movie is over, you'll still have plenty of time left for socializing. For the small price of a video or DVD rental, popcorn, and sodas, you can create a great evening. Perhaps some guests might want to bring appetizers, which will increase the festiveness.

You can also have people over and order in dinner. This will let you serve a nice restaurant meal that takes no preparation time. For fun, serve the meal on nice dishes. While you are paying restaurant prices for the food, you are saving the cost of the tip, as well as the cost of beverages, which easily can amount to as much as the cost of the food.

It is the quality of your friendships and the fun that you have together that makes for an exciting, fulfilling social experience, not how much money you spend. If you have financial goals that require you to save money, schedule activities that create the most fun and add the most to your quality of life while minimizing your expenditures.

69.

Save Money on Your Car Purchase

One of the best ways to save money on a car purchase is to lease a car instead of buying it. Leasing saves money, because at the end of the lease term, you give the car back to the owner, who then can sell it to someone else. That lowers the cost of the car for the person leasing it.

For example, if you buy a $30,000 car and put $2,000 down, your monthly car payment for a forty-eight-month loan will be $644 at five percent interest. However, if you decide to lease that same car, you can expect a significantly lower monthly payment, as well as lower initial payments. With a lease on the same car, you would make a $200 security deposit and a $400 down payment. Already, you have saved $1,400 in up-front costs. A monthly payment at five percent interest for forty-eight months would be $350 a month, which is a savings of $294 a month.

Of course, you will still have a car payment to make each month. Once a lease is up, you will need to sign another lease or purchase the car from the dealer. This situation may not be favorable to some people who look forward to the day that they have no car payment, which immediately puts at least several hundred dollars a month back into the monthly budget.

So what's the right choice? If you have a business where image is really important, then leasing a new car every two to four years may be the best option. Also, if the cost of the lease can be expensed with an employer or deducted from business income, it might make sense to lease. However, if you are budget conscious, the idea of rolling from one lease payment into another may not be appealing. In that case, you might want to purchase the car outright and continue driving it for many years. Even if you don't want to drive the car for many years, by purchasing it, you have it available to resell, which will partially pay for your next car.

The next time that you are shopping for a car, consider a lease in order to minimize your monthly payment. It just might be a favorable financial move.

70.

Save Time with Smart Shopping

In these times, work schedules, family and social commitments, and ordinary errands seem to occupy every minute of our week. Fortunately, we live in a time when there are numerous shopping options that let us purchase exactly what we need in a very time-efficient manner.

One of the best ways to purchase what you need is by mail order. Nearly every store has a companion catalog that sells most of the goods available in the store. Clothes, household furnishings, specialty foods and drinks, and gardening supplies are just a few of the things that you can order over the phone and have shipped directly to the door, eliminating several weekend errands.

While mail order has been around for a long time, the Internet phenomenon has exploded during the last five years or so. There's very little that you can't order on the Internet. Books, CDs, clothes, household and kitchen furnishings, and pet food are just a few of the items that can be purchased online. Both shopping venues can save you money because you may not have to pay sales taxes, depending on what state you live in. If you purchase a minimum amount of goods, you may receive free shipping.

If you have a gift to buy, especially for someone who lives out of town, the Internet or a catalog is a particularly good shopping tactic. You can look at numerous specialty shops in a matter of minutes, which will save you a lot of time compared with driving from store to store. You can have the present wrapped and shipped, further making it a time-efficient way of shopping.

If you aren't technologically oriented or just need to shop for ordinary items, find out if your local retail store will let you order items over the phone and have your purchase delivered. Often, drugstores provide this service, because they have older customers who may not be well enough to come into the store for their purchases. Grocery stores and specialty stores such as pet stores are some other places that may offer delivery.

71.

Choose Your Way to Wealth

Each year, millions of Americans dine out. While restaurants provide a great convenience, a tasty meal, and a night's entertainment, they also can put a dent into the best budget. If you want to build your wealth, try reducing the number of restaurant meals.

Consider the following scenario. If you and your significant other eat out one night a week and pay an average of $60 per meal, that adds up to $3,120 a year. Just by eliminating one restaurant meal every other week, you can save $1,560 a year. For those who aren't afraid to be really frugal, try eliminating most of those meals. Instead, entertain yourself at home. Go to the store and buy some pasta, sauce, and Italian bread and watch your wealth increase.

What you do with that money is just as important as saving it. Wealth creation requires that the saved money be invested. For people with some risk tolerance, stocks can be purchased. A foregone sixty-dollar meal will buy three shares of stock in a restaurant company whose shares trade at twenty dollars. Keep skipping those meals, and soon you will have saved enough to buy 100 shares. For people who are more risk averse, a savings or money market account can be used.

Reducing restaurant meals isn't the only thing that you can do. For instance, try reducing your soda consumption, and watch the savings accumulate. One soda per day at an average cost of $1.50 would save $547.50 a year. Soda lovers who buy two sodas a day would save $1,095 a year. Make a game out of saving your soda money. Each day, take the money that you would have spent on soda, and deposit it into a safe place, such as a drawer or piggy bank. Every other week, take the cash to the bank and deposit it in your savings account. You will be surprised how quickly the balance grows.

Reducing food and soda purchases is an easy and simple way to create wealth without enduring too much suffering. Invest that money, and save your way to wealth.

72.

Selecting the Right Health Plan

Health care is an area of the economy where costs are rising the fastest. Not surprisingly, employers are making numerous changes in their health plans, as well as introducing other plans that lower the costs for both the employer and employee. In order to rest comfortably and know that your health care needs are going to be covered, it is imperative to understand each plan's advantages and disadvantages.

Compare the benefits in your current plan to your new potential plans. To begin this process, write down what benefits you currently have, such as your doctors' visits, prescriptions, and special services that are paid for, such as the chiropractor. Find out whether your current doctors participate in the plans. If they don't, this may be a quick way to eliminate some plans from consideration. Check how much each plan reimburses you for prescriptions that you routinely use. If there is a big discrepancy in what you will have to pay, that obviously will skew your decision.

Next, if you typically use alternative medical services—for instance, if you regularly visit a chiropractor or acupuncturist—you will want to make certain that theses services are covered; otherwise, your expenses can add up quickly. Even though health plans may pay for these services, sometimes they will have a limit on the number of times that they can be accessed. For instance, some insurance plans may limit you to ten or twenty chiropractor visits a year.

Also check whether the plans provide mental health coverage. While you might not plan on checking into a mental health hospital any time soon, you may want to visit a mental health professional at some time. With hourly rates upward of $100 an hour, you will want to make certain that service is covered, even for a half-dozen visits.

What if one plan offers some services but doesn't offer others that you need? The answer is simple. Total up how much money you would spend each month on these services. Whatever is the most expensive service is the one that you should make certain is covered by your health plan. With a little thought and research, it will be easy to choose the right health plan.

73.

Simplify Corporate Earnings Reports

Understanding a quarterly corporate earnings report can be a daunting task, especially with the extensive maze of information that there is to wade through. The secret to working through the maze is understanding exactly what information you are being given and knowing where the hidden information lies.

The most important measure of a company's profitability is earnings. The information is presented in several ways. First, the entire amount of net earnings for the quarter is stated, such as $447 million. Then that amount divided by the number of shares outstanding is given. As an example, the company may have earned $1.70 per share but earned $1.65 per diluted share. The diluted share takes into account what the earnings per share would have been if all of the stock options and convertible securities were exercised.

One of the most confusing things can be when a company reports earnings that are better than what was reported in the same quarter a year earlier (the year earlier quarter) and the share price falls. Although on the surface it seems illogical, it actually isn't. The share price has fallen because even though earnings rose, they did not rise as much as Wall Street institutional investors expected. As a result, investors sold the stock.

Suppose the company met earnings expectations and still sells off after the earnings report comes out? What happened? It could be that even though the net income rose and met expectations, the company warned that the next quarter or the rest of the year would have lower earnings. When comments like that are made, traders sell the stock first and ask questions later. After all, the stock market always looks ahead.

Once you've dissected the net income, look at a company's revenue, or sales, which are used interchangeably. Often, the term "top-line" is used to refer to revenue, because it is the first line on an income statement. Expectations also are formed about revenue. If the actual number falls below expectations, the stock probably will sell off. Declining revenues alone are a reason to sell a stock. If revenues are falling, it is going to be that much harder for companies to maintain their level of profitability.

By understanding a few basic concepts about corporate earnings, you can substantially increase your investing comfort level. If you have knowledge that allows you to read between the lines, you will become a more informed investor who profits from that knowledge.

74.

Take the Bus

While many people who live in rural areas may find that giving up their cars is not feasible, for others it could be possible. Behind a mortgage or rent payment, the car payment is typically the largest monthly expense, especially when the insurance is added in. This expense doesn't even include gasoline and maintenance, which easily can add up to several hundred dollars a month. If you can eliminate that cost, those funds can be used to pay off other bills or be stashed away in your savings account to boost your financial security.

Giving up your car will require you to use other creative ways to get where you need to go. With a little ingenuity, you can probably find alternatives. For instance, how about carpooling to work? If you work at a large company, someone may be going your direction. Perhaps you can take a bus, subway, or train. These options give you the advantage of using the time that you would be driving to have a conversation with a coworker and get to know him or her better. If you are on public transportation, you have the advantage of being able to catch up on your reading or do some work.

If you need a car for errands on the weekend, rent one. On other weekends when you don't have errands, enjoy staying away from the shopping malls and busy suburban roads, which can turn into a traffic jam on a Saturday afternoon that is equivalent to any workday congestion. The price of an infrequent car rental on the weekend will be significantly less than owning your own car.

In addition to reducing your expenses, you also will reduce your stress level by eliminating numerous errands associated with the car. No longer will you have to take the car in for repairs or make appointments to have the oil changed. You will eliminate the time spent washing the car and vacuuming it. Instead, when you do rent a car, it will be cleaned and ready for you.

By opening your mind up to different transportation alternatives, you can simplify your life, create more time, and save money. What better way to make your life easier?

75.

Investing with U.S. Treasuries

Investing your money can be fraught with pitfalls. If you have picked the wrong investments, you possibly face losing your hard-earned money, which could jeopardize your retirement or other financial plans. The concerns can grow if you have invested in the stock market, which sometimes can be extremely volatile.

Fortunately, there is a way around this roller coaster that a risk-averse investor can employ: invest in U.S. Treasuries. Treasuries are backed by the full faith and credit of the U.S. government, which should give even the most nervous investor confidence.

Treasury securities also give investors a range of maturities to match their needs that range from a three-month bill up to a thirty-year bond. Better still, thanks to a program that the Treasury has that enables individual investors to purchase its securities, you can invest in Treasuries with as little as $1,000. Treasury Direct also gives investors another advantage. No commissions are paid, which helps put more of your money to work. It couldn't be easier to purchase the securities. After setting up a Treasury Direct account, you can purchase securities either over the phone or on the Internet.

The Treasury also has other investments targeted at individuals, such as savings bonds and inflation-indexed bonds. I Bonds, as they are called, were created in the late 1990s for investors who want to protect their investments from inflation and be able to earn a guaranteed rate of interest. I Bonds can be purchased in increments of $50, $75, $100, $200, $500, $1,000, $5,000, and $10,000. Interest is added to the bond monthly and paid when the bond is cashed. I Bonds are sold at face value. The interest on I Bonds grows tax-deferred until the bond is cashed in. At that point, federal income taxes must be paid.

Another option for investors is savings bonds sold by the U.S. government. These investments are sold at less than their face value. Upon maturity, the face value of the savings bond is returned to the investor.

The next time that you are feeling anxious about your investments, remove that anxiety by investing in Treasury securities. Then you can relax!

76.

Two Hundred Dollars in Thirty Minutes

Time is money—we've all heard that saying hundreds of times. However, time also can produce money, if you take the time to shop around and compare prices before purchasing.

Comparison shopping is a wise strategy for people who are committed to having the life that they want, filled with many fun activities while achieving important financial goals. Suppose that you want to take a trip from Los Angeles to Miami. Many airlines fly this route and charge a wide variety of prices. You could pay several thousand dollars for a first-class ticket, or you could spend a little time and attempt to find the cheapest alternative. If you have important financial goals that require funding, the wise person will look for bargains in order to make certain that he or she has the money available to fund other important financial goals.

When you first begin pricing the ticket, you may find one that costs $500. With a few more calls or Internet searches, it is quite likely that ticket price will be reduced to $300 or so, saving you

$200 after spending only about thirty extra minutes. If you are flexible with your schedule, you can find further savings by using a service such as Priceline.com that allows you to offer what price you want to pay for an airline ticket.

Comparing prices before you purchase large consumer items such as a television is very important. Just by visiting several stores and calling others, you probably will end up saving a considerable amount of money. There are also many powerful search engines on the Internet that can help you find the best price available for a product—or you can use the Internet to check out prices at individual stores instead of driving there or calling.

Few people have surplus money. However, everyone wants to achieve his or her financial goals and maximize the money that is available. With that in mind, it is worth your effort to shop around and make certain that you are getting the best price possible. If thirty minutes' worth of work will put $200 in your pocket, you have nothing to lose and everything to gain.

77.

Spend Your Way to Wealth

Sometimes, we rebel against reining in our spending. After all, we work hard, and we are entitled to a few luxuries. What's the point, if you can't enjoy some of your hard-earned money? The good news is that you don't have to rein in your spending. Instead, consider where you are spending your money.

Instead of buying a video game console, why not buy shares of a company that makes one of the popular ones? Several years after you've lost interest in your purchase, you will still have an investment that may appreciate and pay dividends.

What about those magazines that you purchase frequently? Instead of spending money at the newsstand, purchase shares of companies that publish the magazines. If you really need to read the magazine, you can probably read it at the library. Many magazines also have a significant number of their articles available online that aren't password protected.

Clothes are another popular item that soon become outdated and discarded. The next time that you see a good deal on a shirt—

especially one that you don't really need—save your money, and spend it on shares of a retail company that sells the shirt.

Instead of spending money on household products or new gadgets that will soon be used up or that aren't really needed, purchase shares in discount chains. While electronic gadgets, such as digital cameras, handheld organizers, or the newest cell phones, are useful, within ten months, there likely will be a newer, more up-to-date version of the product available. How about spending your money on purchasing shares of the companies that sell those products? You can always buy those products later when the new and updated versions are available.

It's not just about how much money you spend, but also where you spend your money. Make certain that you are spending your money wisely and spending it toward creating wealth.

78.

Keep to Your Budget

Once you have taken the positive step of setting financial goals and committing to accomplishing them, it is time to make certain that you take the appropriate actions to achieve them. One important tool is setting up a budget.

Just because you are keeping track of what you are spending doesn't mean that the task has to be difficult. You can use either a paper-based system or a computer software program to help you. Either way, the end result will put you on the road to achieving your goals and being true to your commitments.

If you are using software, the first task is to purchase a financial management software program designed for individuals. Once it is installed, you are ready to go. You will have to allow some time to set up the program, which includes entering information about your bank and credit card balances.

Once that is done, use the program to record checks that you've written. When you receive your monthly statement, you can use the program to balance your checking account, which saves time. Your balance is automatically calculated for you. You can also use this to track spending. These tools allow you to fulfill the most important commitments that you have—the ones to yourself.

A software program also can help you achieve your goals by making it easy to keep track of all of those coffees or lunches that you spend a few dollars on which, over time, add up to a significant expenditure. In order to track these small expenses, start saving the receipts and recording them in the software.

If you don't feel comfortable with computers, don't worry. The same goals can be accomplished using a pencil and paper. Start writing down what you spend under which categories, such as rent, utilities, clothing, and cash expenditures. At the end of the week or month, total up everything in each category.

Whatever method you choose, the important thing is that you have begun to take positive steps to increase your quality of life and inner peace by tracking your spending and making certain that you can meet your financial goals. Rather than being a burden, the sole purpose of your budget is to empower yourself to reach your goals and achieve a terrific quality of life.

79.

Stop Paying So Many Bills!

Reducing the number of monthly bills that you receive sounds like a dream come true. Here's how to accomplish that and pay only "two" bills a month.

Each day, when you receive your bills, put them in one spot where you can easily find them. For the first month when the bills arrive, you will have to open them to see when the due date is. If you plan to pay your "first" bill on the fifteenth of the month, you will have to make certain that allows plenty of time for the companies to receive your checks.

Now, clear your desk, retrieve your checkbook, and then begin paying your bills. Within fifteen to thirty minutes, you will be done and "one" of your monthly bills will be paid.

When the second bill payment date arrives, repeat the process. This technique will make it seem like you have only "two" bills to pay because all of the work surrounding paying bills is restricted to twice a month.

80.

Use Direct Debit

Set up direct debits with your creditors. This way, you can at least save time, even if you still have to pay your bill. Many companies will let you fill out a form to have the amount of the bill debited, or deducted, from your checking account. Each month, a statement is mailed to you showing the amount of charges that you have incurred and showing that the bill has been paid with money from your checking account. Once you receive the statement in the mail, you can review it and make certain that everything is in order. Then you file the bill away, and you're finished. You don't have any bills to pay!

If there is a problem with any bill, you can contact the company and ask them to fix the problem. The company should quickly cooperate, because it wants to retain your trust. Credit card companies, telephone companies, apartment managers, and mortgage providers are some of the creditors that want their customers to pay their bills by direct debit. They are assured that the bills will get paid, and it saves them the time of processing the check, reducing their costs.

Direct debit is just as good for the consumer as it is for the company. Few people have any extra time to spend paying bills. Why not save the time and trouble of writing and mailing a check for ordinary expenses such as the cable, electric, or telephone bills that are virtually the same each month?

Direct debit also removes a problem for the person who isn't very organized and sometimes pays his or her bills late, even though there is plenty of money in the checking account. For the organizationally challenged, direct debit offers a perfect solution that saves time, eliminates bills being paid late, and is bound to make you and your creditors happy.

81.

Gourmet Meals on a Budget

There's nothing better than a tasty meal and a great bottle of wine—and you can have your gourmet meal without having to pay inflated prices. It's very easy to find several recipes that don't take too much time or require professional training at a culinary institute to be successful.

Pizzas don't require any more effort than assembling ingredients on top of a crust. If the recipe calls for homemade dough, skip that part, and instead buy a frozen crust in the grocery store. You may spend seven to ten dollars on ingredients and then purchase a bottle of soda or wine for two to twelve dollars. The total cost of your dinner will range from nine to twenty-two dollars. Divide that by four people, and you have spent $5.50 a person for dinner. Even the average fast food dinner or sandwich will cost more than that. Compare the cost of the pizza dinner with the same meal in a restaurant, which might be as much as fifty dollars, or double what your home-cooked meal cost.

Pasta dishes also offer an easy and delicious alternative to a restaurant meal. They typically aren't difficult to make and are a great way to serve a group of people. Add a small salad and a simple vegetable, and you are done. For the summer, try just an elegant salad, which requires little more than assembling ingredients, or purchase some meat or fish, make a light sauce, add a small garden salad, and you are done. In the winter, soups offer a tasty and very inexpensive way to cook a meal.

Look at food magazines, cookbooks, and the Internet for recipes. You can find virtually any recipe for any type of occasion online. Watch for recipes targeted at beginners or those that say they are quick and easy. Make certain that the recipes don't have too many ingredients, because lengthy recipes tend to be more complex—and more expensive. Read through a recipe to judge whether it is something that you can do.

With just a little time and planning, you can preserve your budget and have a good time in the process. Cooking more will excite your taste buds—and your wallet.

82.

Teach Your Children to Be Wealthy

One of the most important things that parents can do is to teach their children how to save money. While that may sound old-fashioned, keeping more money than you spend creates wealth. You've heard of older people who don't appear to be well-to-do. When they die and their estates are settled, many people are shocked to find out that they actually were worth several million dollars, despite never earning a huge salary. That is the power of saving.

That scenario stresses the importance of investments. While you can build wealth by saving money, if you really want to increase your assets, you must invest your money well. Parents can help their children by setting up their own brokerage accounts and letting them select stocks or mutual funds. By providing your children with a supportive environment in which to learn, you will be giving them valuable lessons.

Encourage your children to refrain from spending everything they make so that they have money to invest. In order to communicate this lesson to your children, they need to understand the value of a dollar. There are several ways that this can be taught. Perhaps you will require your children to have a part-time job during teenage years in order to comprehend how difficult it can be to make money.

Alternatively, by giving children an allowance, they will see just how quickly money can be spent and experience how slowly it can come in. While that is a sobering lesson, it is a valuable one based in reality, as any adult can verify.

If money comes in relatively slowly, another lesson to show your children is how to plan for large purchases. Too often, people don't want to wait to buy what they want. They immediately charge a purchase, building a credit card balance in the process. That isn't financially healthy. Help your children avoid falling into that trap by teaching them to set aside money for large purchases. With a few simple lessons, you can make certain that your children are educated about finances.

83.

Teach Your Teen the Value of a Dollar

There are several strategies that you can use to teach your teenagers about the value of a dollar. Probably one of the best ways is to let them get jobs. Obviously, they will be working for an hourly wage that is relatively modest as they turn to a retail store or fast-food business for a paycheck, or to providing child care, pet care, or lawn-mowing services. After a hard week or two of work, let them experience the expectation of getting a "large" sum of money, only to have it diluted by the amount of taxes and Social Security that is withheld. This can be a sobering experience. If your children didn't understand the value of a dollar before those paychecks arrived, they soon will.

Perhaps you don't want your children to spend time working when they could be studying, participating in activities that will help their chances of getting into the colleges of their choice, or socializing with their peers. In that case, you can give your children an allowance that they have to use for their entertainment expenses, clothing, and gifts for friends. As long as this allowance isn't unlimited, they will soon see how far it does or doesn't go.

If either one of those methods isn't going to work, set your children up in an imaginary household. Let them pretend that they have graduated from college, found jobs in their intended professions, and received the average amount of pay. Challenge them to figure out how much their take-home pay will be, and then use this to rent an apartment, or even contemplate buying a house. While at first glance, that salary may seem quite large, it soon will shrink as the reality of paying rent, utilities, groceries, car expenses, and entertainment sinks in.

Every parent wants to give his or her children the best advantages possible. Sometimes, however, including a dose of reality with those advantages can be a winning strategy. Even though your children may have better economic circumstances than you did, there is no reason why they can't have a bird's-eye view of the value of a dollar.

84.

Do I Really Need This?

Staying within the limits of your budget can seem about as challenging as climbing Mount McKinley. However, it doesn't have to be. Sometimes, all it takes is asking yourself, "Do I really need this?"

By asking yourself if you really need to make a purchase, quite often, if you are truthful, the answer will come back as "no." If you declare that you don't need to buy something, that stops you from attempting to figure out if you have money in your budget. It also prevents you from possibly putting a purchase on an already overburdened credit card.

Americans excel in many areas, and one of those is shopping and spending money. Retail stores have helped encourage shopping habits as they seek to increase sales and profits. They take out advertisements with celebrity endorsements to push designer goods that you "have to have." Banks also have done their part by sending out millions of "pre-approved" credit card applications to increase usage of their credit cards.

There is nothing that says that you have to give in to this pressure. After all, you don't want these people to brainwash you. Just saying those simple words, "Do I really need this?" can stop consumer pressure dead in its tracks.

For instance, imagine that you are in a department store on a Saturday afternoon, and you are in the television section. All of the sudden, a thirty-percent-off sign catches your eye. It is a big-screen TV that you've had your eye on for a long time. The price looks much better, but it is still more than you can really afford. You know that if you wait another year or so, new technology will be developed and prices probably will be lower. Now, the question of whether you really need the television comes in handy.

Remember, it is your money and your responsibility alone to determine how you spend it. No other person can control what you do. If you really want and need to buy something and it fits into your budget, then by all means, go ahead. For those other purchases that are not essential or important, learn how to say no.

85.

The Miracle of Saving

A larger savings account will automatically give you more options in any time of need. Beyond covering big, unexpected expenses, a savings account will allow you to pay for pleasant events, as well. By having a savings account, you will be able to make spur-of-the-moment financial decisions without putting yourself in debt.

To obtain these benefits, you will need to start saving. If you put $100 a month away for three years and the money is invested at four percent, you will have $3,931 at the end of the three years. That's not bad for starting out with $100 three years earlier.

However, if you invest $1,000 in a three-year CD paying four percent, by the end of that time period you will have $4,945, thanks to the power of compound interest. An initial $1,000 investment will deliver more money after three years, but do whatever you can manage. The important thing is to begin saving.

Think what power the miracle of savings can do for you and your financial and emotional well-being.

86.

Time Is Money—Really

Everyone has heard the saying, "Time is money," but now more than ever, that statement rings true. While we often think that we are being frugal and saving money by cleaning our own houses, changing the oil in our cars, or cooking meals, the truth is that you should value your free time at the same level that your employer pays you to work.

Depending on your individual salary and your cost of living, you should determine whether you should do tasks yourself or hire someone to complete them. To begin your calculations, you will need to find out your hourly pay rate. To do that, divide your annual salary by fifty-two weeks, and then divide that number by forty hours or the number of hours that you actually work. Now, you have your hourly rate, and this gives you an idea of what your free time should be worth to you.

Next, make a list of tasks that you do that seem to take an inordinate amount of your time. Next to each task, write down how much time you spend doing it. For instance, if you spend five hours cleaning the house, and your hourly rate is $27.88 an hour, it costs you a total of $139.40. (You may take longer because you are distracted or spend time straightening—things that a professional cleaner wouldn't necessarily do.) Suppose you can hire someone at twenty dollars an hour for four hours—a total cost of eighty dollars. Just by hiring someone, you can save $59.40. Remember, your time is worth money.

Similar savings may be gained by analyzing how much time you spend preparing meals. If you want to make lasagna, that may take one and a half hours. At $27.88 an hour, that would cost $41.82. You probably can purchase lasagna cheaper at the deli counter of your local grocery store or as takeout from a restaurant. However, if you want to make a spaghetti dinner, you may find that you can prepare everything in less than a half-hour. In that case, you probably would save money by preparing your own meal.

By the same token, if changing the oil takes you a half-hour, it will cost you $13.94. If a garage charges thirty dollars, then it is worth it for you to change your own oil.

There are no right or wrong answers when it comes to deciding whether to hire someone to provide a service or to do it yourself. Instead, do your own calculations and find the right answer for you.

87.

Rent Your Home for the Summer

Depending on where you live, rents can range from several thousand dollars a week up to $50,000 to $70,000 per month for waterfront houses in seaside communities. While not everyone will earn $70,000 a month for their property, most people could earn at least $10,000 during the summer. That's not a bad way to bolster your finances.

Don't think that you have to own a mansion in order to rent your house. Most people who rent a home want to stay right on the waterfront, and they are more concerned about the location. They don't necessarily need as much space as they have in their own homes. If your house is clean and neat, that is the most important selling point. Even if your house isn't near the beach, if you live in the mountains or a popular golfing area, there still may be an opportunity to rent your house.

Of course, if another family is living in your house, you have to be creative to figure out where you will live for the summer. In some cases, families may go visit relatives. Others charge a significant fee to rent their houses and then rent other accommodations for less money, making a profit in the process. A cross-country car trip might be another option. Some people may combine these strategies in order to put a roof over their heads for the summer months. For summer landlords whose towns are besieged by summer tourists or beachgoers, getting away from the traffic and congestion alone may feel like a wonderful vacation, even without going to a splashy, popular destination.

While renting out your home may not be a desirable strategy for everyone, it is one way that you can utilize your present financial resources to make more money. Your summer rental plan can then allow you to fund some of life's luxuries—or necessities, such as your children's college education or your retirement. Explore whether renting out your home will work for you. It just may provide the financial windfall that you have been seeking.

88.

Eight Hundred Dollars for Pennies

You can create $800 at the end of a year just by saving your change. Set aside a large jar or series of jars. Each day, when you arrive at home, empty your pockets or your coin purse, and put the change in the jar. You won't miss the money. By dropping the coins into the jar, you can see and hear the accomplishment of a goal, which gives you positive reinforcement that you are working on your savings.

Saving $800 a year requires only saving fifteen dollars a week. That amount works out to just a little more than two dollars a day—a sum that few people will ever miss.

If you don't like the idea of collecting change, you can alter the process slightly. Most people can cut out one soda or a cup of coffee during the day to produce some savings. To reinforce your savings plan, take the saved money and put it in a glass jar.

Today, most people don't even bother to bend down and pick up a penny off the street. They should, because each penny can lead to a nice nest egg at the end of the year.

89.

Wiping Out Your Credit Card Balance

Paying for purchases with credit cards has become easier than ever. Unfortunately, so has quickly ringing up credit card balances, thanks to large interest charges. There are a few things that you can do to make certain that credit card debt doesn't pile up on you.

After making a purchase, write down the amount of the charge in a visible place that you frequently see. Total that expenditure with the other ones that have been made that month. This allows you to know exactly how much money you owe on your card and to be prepared to pay it when the bill comes. If you've spent $600, and you know that is the most that you can afford, stop using your card.

If keeping track of the expenditures isn't sufficient to stop your spending, you may need to try a different tactic. At the end of each week, write a check to the credit card company that equals the total of your charge purchases. Deduct that amount from your checking account. Do this every week, and when the bill comes, you will have your checks ready to be mailed in order to pay the bill.

If these strategies aren't going to work, you may need to try something that is more aggressive. Many credit card companies offer secured credit cards that require you to put money on deposit. If you deposit $1,000, you have a credit limit of $1,000. If you charge $800, then you only have $200 left on your card until you pay the balance. Once you've reached the limit, your expenditures are stopped, eliminating the risk that you will overspend. Often, people who are a bad credit risk obtain these cards, because these are the only types of credit cards that they can get. Because you have "secured" your payments with your initial deposit, there is little risk for the lender.

Finally, there is one other way to instill discipline into your credit card shopping practices. Obtain an American Express card that requires you to pay off your balance in full each month. With such a card, you don't have any other choice.

Every financial situation has various options. Make certain that you find an option that is appropriate for you and makes it easy for you to keep your credit card spending in check.

90.

Understanding Mutual Funds

Mutual funds may sound like a complicated investment. However, by understanding a few basic concepts, you can turn them into an investment that you thoroughly understand.

The best place to start is the price of the mutual fund. Instead of being straightforward, the industry uses the term "net asset value" (NAV). At the end of each trading day, the NAV is calculated by using the closing price of the investment and then totaling the net assets of the fund, which is divided by the number of shares outstanding.

The next important thing to understand is what investments a mutual fund will make. For instance, a fund may invest in stocks of large-cap, or large, companies, or it may invest in small-cap, or smaller, companies. A mutual fund also may have a much narrower focus and invest only in shares of biotech companies, or perhaps companies involved in gold mining.

You should know the difference between a growth fund and a value fund. Growth funds purchase stocks that have above-average growth potential and likely won't pay dividends. If you need current income, invest in a value fund, which pays above-average dividends.

Other mutual funds may invest only in bonds and perhaps restrict their investment activity to bonds with long- or short-term maturities. Other bond funds may mix the different maturities.

In terms of cost, the first fee that you'll need to know about is the sales charge, or load, that the fund has. Often, this will range from one percent to about five percent and be charged on the money invested. For instance, if you invest $1,000 in a mutual fund with a five percent load, you will actually invest $950 into the mutual fund. Fifty dollars will be deducted by the mutual fund in order to pay the sales charge. In contrast, no-load funds don't have any charge, but that doesn't mean that they are free of costs. No-load funds assess annual fund operating expenses. These will be stated as a percentage, such as 0.50 percent, and are deducted from the fund's assets. Typically, the fee is divided into three subcategories: management expenses; a 12b-1 distribution fee, which pays for marketing expenses; and an "other expense" category.

By understanding a few basic definitions and characteristics about mutual funds, you can begin to learn more and take control of your finances. A little knowledge is all you need.

91.

As Good as Gold

We've all heard the saying, "As good as gold," but what does that really mean? For investors, gold is viewed as a safe investment. Gold has served as a store of currency since the early days of civilization. It retains its value, unlike paper-based currencies, which can become worthless from rapidly rising inflation. Currencies also can be cancelled by governments, which wipes out all financial wealth.

Not surprisingly, during periods of declining stock markets, economic or political turbulence, or deflation, people begin to turn to gold as a safe-haven investment. If you are a very cautious investor, and you want to protect your money from economic turmoil, you may want to allocate some of your investments into gold.

This phenomenon is frequently observed. If the stock market falls dramatically, the price of gold will rise as investors take some of their money out of stocks and transfer it into gold. Also, if the value of the U.S. dollar falls sharply, gold prices often will rise sharply.

During political turmoil, times of war, or other conflicts, the price of gold also will rise sharply. For instance, gold prices jumped sharply in the months leading up to the Iraqi conflict that began in March 2003. Once the market judged that the worst was over, the price of gold slid. This situation has been repeated many times.

In developing countries, such as India or the Middle East, people will buy gold jewelry as a way to safeguard some of their money. While a currency or the value of an investment may fall drastically, gold jewelry typically holds its value and can be sold or used to purchase goods, just like a currency.

In the United States, gold investments are made through the purchase of either gold coins or gold bars, which require a significant amount of money. Typically, governments issue gold coins, called bullion coins. Coins also may be made by private businesses, often in smaller quantities. Once sold, they may trade at a markup to their gold content that places a higher value on aesthetics. Some popular gold coins include the American Eagle, the Canadian Maple Leaf, the South African Krugerrand, and the China Mint Panda Bear.

For investors who believe that the world is a risky place and want to make certain that they can sleep at night, gold may be a good investment. After all, what is the point of having money if you are too stressed to enjoy it?

92.

Use a Reverse Mortgage

A reverse mortgage is a useful way for a rich homeowner who is cash poor to put extra money into his or her bank account. Reverse mortgages give homeowners with a substantial amount of home equity the ability to draw out money from their house. In a reverse mortgage, the bank puts a mortgage on the house and gives the owner the proceeds of the mortgage, instead of giving the money to the counter-party selling the house, which would happen in a normal real estate transaction. In effect, the owner is selling the house to the bank. The payments can be paid monthly or in a lump sum, or accessed through a line of credit.

The typical person who receives a reverse mortgage is older, with a house that has substantially risen in value. However, despite owning an expensive house, the reverse mortgagee probably has little cash in the bank and is mostly relying on a Social Security check or a fixed pension payment. The money from the reverse mortgage that is borrowed usually doesn't have to be paid until after the death of the mortgagee. Then the house is sold and the bank is repaid.

There's the saying, "You can't take it with you." The truth of that is not lost on retired people who are barely keeping their heads above water financially, even though they live in a sharply appreciated home in a trendy area. A reverse mortgage allows the owner to benefit from the appreciation of the house without having to sell it and move out.

A reverse mortgage won't exceed the value of the house. If there are heirs that the homeowner wants to bequeath his or her assets to, then the heirs will still probably receive some money, especially if the homeowner receives the payout from the reverse mortgage monthly. Depending on how long the person lives, the total amount paid out may be a very small amount.

The popularity of reverse mortgages has substantially increased in recent years, as more people become familiar with the concept. As the real estate market continues to rise, houses in many communities have sharply increased in value, turning once-modest middle-class houses into expensive houses, even though they may still be modest in appearance.

93.

Use Asset Allocation

Very simply, asset allocation is a technique that lets you decide what percentage of your investment portfolio should be allocated to stocks, bonds, other asset classes, or cash. Finance professionals put a lot of belief in getting the asset allocation right— they believe that this determines the return that the portfolio earns more than anything else.

Your willingness to take on risk will determine how much money you should invest in stocks. Younger investors who have many years until retirement may feel like heavily concentrating in stocks—perhaps as much as eighty-five or ninety percent. Equity allocations that high may make sense if you believe that the stock market is likely to rise.

However, for someone who is risk averse, the amount allocated to stocks will be significantly less. Over time, equities are expected to have a higher return than other investments, but they also have more risk. Risk-averse people are willing to forego some return in order to limit their risk and may only have forty to seventy percent of their portfolios in equities.

Once you set the allocation for equities, you can determine how much you want to invest in fixed-income securities such as bonds. If your equity allocation is eighty percent, you might have fifteen percent in fixed income and the remainder in cash. Similarly, a risk-averse investor may have fifty percent of his or her allocation in equities—forty percent in fixed income and ten percent in cash.

Once you set up your asset allocation plan and realign your portfolio so that you have the right mix, you will have to periodically rebalance the portfolio. This means that once or twice a year, you will need to reexamine how much of your portfolio is in equities and bonds. The amounts will vary as income, such as interest and dividend payments, flows in and prices rise and fall. If you have too much in equities, you will need to sell some of your stocks. If your equity percentage has decreased, you will need to buy additional shares.

The advantage of asset allocation is that it can help reduce your risk and optimize your potential return, because a strategic mix of asset classes is used, which produces diversification. Through diversification, investors can reduce the negative impact when there is a downturn in one asset class.

94.

Credit Cards for Organization

There are only a few things that you can't pay for using a credit card. With that in mind, you can use your credit card for many different purchases. When the statement comes, you can input the charges into your personal financial software program. That lets you track your expenses and make certain that you aren't spending too much money. If you aren't keen on that idea but still need to know where you spent your money, especially at tax time, many credit card companies mail their customers end-of-the-year breakdowns, showing how much they spent on travel, retail shops, or dining establishments.

Credit cards also can be useful to help entrepreneurs keep their business expenditures separate from personal expenses. For instance, business lunches, travel expenses, office supply purchases, and work-related auto expenses can be paid for using a credit card. At the end of the year, when you are preparing your financial information to go to the accountant, you know that anything on this card is business related. Then it becomes a simple matter of copying twelve credit card statements and handing them to your accountant, who can easily classify those expenses.

Another way that credit cards are useful is that they provide a record of your purchases that can be helpful when it comes to returning unwanted goods. If you lose the receipt, you know that the purchase has been logged on your statement.

While credit cards can make your life, and your necessary bookkeeping, significantly easier, they also can land you in debt if they aren't used correctly. If you use your credit cards like cash or checks to pay for expenses, just make certain that you pay off the balance each month. Otherwise, the credit card's ability to help you organize your finances will soon turn into a plot to wreck your financial well-being. Remember, you want to reduce the stress in your life, not increase it. Don't turn your credit cards from an advantage into a problem.

95.

Use Debt to Get Out of Debt

If you have a credit card balance or a car loan with a high interest rate, these are some of the most expensive forms of consumer debt. Much less expensive is a home equity line of credit, especially since the interest rate on mortgages dropped to record low levels in 2003.

Eliminate your high-interest rate debt and pay those credit cards with your home equity line of credit. The advantage of using a home equity line of credit to pay off your credit card balance or other high-interest debt is that you save money by locking in a lower interest rate and lowering your payments. That enables you to pay off the debt at a much faster pace and save money.

A home equity line of credit has another substantial benefit. Because the credit line is connected to your home, the interest paid can be deducted from the amount of income tax owed. While you still have to pay interest, at least it is helping you lower the amount of income taxes that you pay. In contrast, interest paid on credit cards or automobiles is not tax deductible.

You also may use a home equity line of credit to renovate or redecorate a kitchen or bathroom. While it isn't a good thing to have too much debt, using a home equity loan to pay for improvements to the house that will increase its resale value is a good use of the funds. A home equity line of credit avoids using a high-interest credit card to pay for home improvement expenses and lowers your overall cost and debt level.

Additionally, using a home equity line of credit to consolidate your bills has the added advantage of simplifying your debt situation, and perhaps making you more aware of what you have to pay each month. For instance, if you are paying three or four credit cards a month, the minimum payment for each will be smaller and may provide the illusion that you don't have that much debt. By grouping everything together, the illusion of less debt will be harder to sustain and the higher minimum payment will reinforce the fact that you do have a debt to pay.

Next time that you end up with too much debt, think about finding a lower cost debt source in order to help you take control of the situation. You'll be glad that you did.

96.

Set Your Children on the
Right Financial Path

It's a timeworn saying that you should save money for a rainy day. However, why not focus on the positive and save money for important goals and projects that will allow you to lead the life that you want?

For instance, suppose that you've always dreamed of taking a trip around the world. While that sounds like a brilliant idea that everyone would want to do, the reality is that for many people, it wouldn't be possible. Job considerations and lack of money would be two impediments. However, just because there are impediments doesn't mean that you have to let them stop you.

One of the easiest things to manage is money. If you really want to take a once-in-a-lifetime trip, why not start saving for it now? Set aside a small but sufficient amount of money into a savings account, and watch your balance build. If family and friends want to give you a present for your birthday or the holidays but don't know what to give, suggest that they give you a small donation for your trip.

You can also use this technique to instill values in your children. For instance, why not have your children begin saving some of their money for important expenses in their lives? These may be the down payment for a house, the purchase price of a new car, or a special event such as a wedding or honeymoon. Positively teach your children that if they want something big and expensive, the way to obtain it is by saving their money.

Help older teenagers who have part-time jobs to open up IRAs and deposit some of their earnings into them. By getting them in the habit of setting aside some of their income for retirement early on, you will be teaching them an important lesson for their entire lives.

Saving for a rainy day is prudent advice. It is prudent to save for the best days of your life, too!

97.

Picking Winning Stocks

Whether you realize it or not, you have a great deal of expertise that enables you to pick winning stocks. It isn't necessary to hold an MBA or to have managed a portfolio for ten years or longer.

Some of the people who knew earliest that Wal-Mart Corporation would be a success were homemakers living in the South. Long before Wal-Mart appeared in the national spotlight, they continued to spend more of their shopping dollars at Wal-Mart. If you are attempting to pick some retail stocks that you want to invest in, what better recommendations for companies than your shopping habits and those of your friends?

The homemaker living in a small, rural town in the South in the 1970s was probably better informed about Wal-Mart than the stock-picking experts back East. There are plenty of similar opportunities today to recognize which companies are thriving and which aren't.

For example, if you want to gauge which restaurant chain is likely to succeed, just drive by the parking lots of several different restaurants on different days throughout the week and compare how crowded they are. Better yet, call to see if you can get a reservation or find out how long the wait is to determine which restaurants are likely to thrive and which aren't.

Young adults also have their areas of expertise, such as knowing what the latest fashion and music trends are. If you want to know what products and clothing will be a success with teenagers, just ask them. They have a clear idea of what is hot and what is out-of-fashion. Once you have the basic marketing information, it is just a small calculation to determine what companies sell those products and which ones are supposed to be most successful.

People who are home repair enthusiasts or automobile buffs are in a great position to be able to spot trends, as well as up-and-coming companies. Remember, at one point, Home Depot was a small chain that had yet to be fully recognized.

Regardless of our education or training, we all have our areas of expertise. When it comes to picking stocks, put your expertise to use. While you may not have the formal business training of other so-called experts, in many instances, you may be better-positioned to pick the next stock winner than some of them.

98.

The Dollar's Strength

In the latter half of the 1990s, the United States had a "strong" dollar. Beginning in 2003, economists began to talk about a "weak" dollar. What does that mean for you?

If you love imported goods, such as French wine, Swiss chocolates, foreign cars, and international fashion, and the dollar weakens, this means that the price that you will pay for those goods will rise. As the value of the dollar falls against other currencies, it takes more dollars to buy the equivalent euro, Swiss franc, or Japanese yen. This means that you will have to pay more dollars in order to buy euros that can be used to pay for your imported purses and clothes.

For instance, when the dollar was trading against the euro at $0.88, it only took eighty-eight cents to buy one euro. When the euro strengthened to $1.17, it required $1.17 to purchase one euro. At $1.17, the dollar has fallen in value by thirty-three percent against the euro. All other things being equal, goods made by European companies that have adopted the euro would now cost about one-third more.

If the dollar is weak, it makes foreign vacations more expensive for the same reason. More dollars will be required to purchase euros to pay for that Paris hotel and dinner at the restaurant at the Eiffel Tower.

A weakening dollar means that consumers will probably alter some of their spending habits. Increasingly, American-made goods can be expected to gain in popularity as their relative price decreases. Americans also may begin to shift some of their purchases to domestic goods and begin to explore vacation alternatives that are a lot closer to home.

In contrast, a strong dollar means that it takes fewer U.S. dollars to buy foreign currencies. The price of foreign goods and vacations becomes less expensive for Americans.

The value of changing currencies has a much more substantial effect on American businesses. A weakening dollar reduces the cost of American goods that are exported to other companies, which helps drive up demand for U.S. products overseas. Also, the goods produced by U.S. companies look more attractive at home, because the relative price of imported goods has risen. As a result, U.S. companies may find that their sales are rising, which could prompt them to hire more workers, benefiting the overall economy.

A rising or falling dollar isn't necessarily bad or good. Instead, it depends upon your role in the transaction and your understanding the part that you play in world economics.

99.

Spend Money to Improve
Your Quality of Life

We all spend many hundreds, if not thousands, of dollars each month. Why not spend some of this money on things that will improve the quality of your life? While you can't stop paying the rent or your car payment, there is no reason why you can't make certain that at least a small percentage of your income is spent on activities or projects that will dramatically increase your quality of life.

For instance, why not spend money to start a garden or upgrade an existing one? This activity can provide relaxation and an opportunity to be outside, especially in the springtime when everything is blooming and the world feels fresh. A garden can give you a healthy pickup and bring joy and beauty into your life. A garden also will give you a sense of accomplishment, because you have made something beautiful.

There are other options, as well. Instead of taking on a project, you might want to do something that is much less energy-intensive, such as taking a yoga class. Yoga instruction helps you relax and increases your flexibility. During the class, you are constantly cautioned against straining yourself or competing against other people.

Other short-term community classes might also add to your life. It might be fun to do something out of the ordinary, such as taking a tap dancing class or a drawing class.

You obviously will continue paying your major bills and funding your savings and retirement accounts. However, make certain that you allocate a few dollars each month to activities that will improve your quality of life, whether they give you more peace and relaxation, get you outside into the fresh air, or teach you a new skill or hobby.

100.
Your Will

Even if you aren't wealthy, it is still a very good idea to write a will directing how you want your assets dispersed and your debts paid off. If you die without a will, the government of the state that you live in will decide how your assets are divided, and you just might not be pleased with the outcome.

Don't leave anything to chance. Wills allow you to leave directions about paying off debts such as mortgages or car loans. In a will, you also will be able to designate where your money goes—to a spouse, children, family members, close friends, or a charity. The will should say who should receive different personal property, such as clothes, furniture, jewelry, or artwork, as well.

Within the will, you will be able to designate who should implement all of your decisions. This person is known as an executor. It may be a family member, close friend, or attorney. A second person also is chosen as a backup, in case the first person is unavailable or unable to carry out the duties.

Wills are particularly important for people with children. The will identifies who will be the children's legal guardian if both spouses die. While it is an unpleasant process to determine who should be successive parents, it is extremely important. If you don't designate who should raise your children, the state will determine this for you.

Many attorneys charge modest, flat fees ranging from $300 to $1,000 to prepare a simple will, which will take care of the needs of many people. The process shouldn't take more than several weeks, assuming that you know how you want everything to be divided. For others who feel that they have some legal knowledge and really want to take matters into their own hands, there are other options, such as using an online service to create your own will. Books or preprinted forms also are helpful.

Whatever option you choose, it is important that you have a will. Otherwise, you've given up your say about how your assets should be divided, which may cause additional problems for your friends and family beyond mourning your death.